FOUNDATIONS

PEACE · LOVE · HOPE · JOY

A Parent's Introduction to
Christian Education

Kenneth J. Kremer

NORTHWESTERN PUBLISHING HOUSE
Milwaukee, Wisconsin

*To all whose passion is
to bring children to Jesus*

Cover Illustration: Shutterstock
Art Director: Karen Knutson
Designer: Pamela Dunn

Northwestern Publishing House
1250 N. 113th St., Milwaukee, WI 53226-3284
www.nph.net
© 2013 by Northwestern Publishing House
Published 2013
Printed in the United States of America
ISBN 978-0-8100-2475-5

FOUNDATIONS

A Parent's Introduction to
Christian Education

CONTENTS

Part Three: JOY

Part Four: LOVE

"The foundations of the earth are the LORD's;
upon them he has set the world."

1 SAMUEL 2:8

FOREWORD

This book is written for parents. It discusses things about schools and learning that parents are talking about with other parents. The topic is education or, more specifically, *educational models*. Before you dismiss the book as academic, you should know that it is different from other books on the subject. Its purpose is to help you see the importance of the vital role you play in your child's education. As the subtitle says, it is a *parent's introduction*.

You already care about the kind of education your child receives. Good parents do. You understand that the interest you take in your child's education will lead to some of the most exciting and important decisions you will ever make. Experience has taught you that having a quality education is critical in today's world. This book will help you focus on the things that matter most when it comes to achieving the objectives you have set for your child's education. It has been written in language that any parent can understand. No jargon. No hype. It's not a policy handbook or a book of rules and regulations. Nor is it a marketing ploy to promote Lutheran schools. It speaks to the important issues that every parent deals with during the schooling years. It does so directly, honestly, and with clarity. The aim is to help you navigate the unique approach to learning that we will be referring to as *Christian education*. You will be empowered to take a proactive role in influencing your child's future. You will discover *how* Christian education works, *why* it works, and why it will prove to be one of the most valuable gifts you can ever give your child. Along the way you will begin to see a clear distinction between the secular educational model and the Christian educational model. The differences will at first seem more theoretical than practical. As you delve deeper into the foundational principles of Christian education, you will begin to recognize that Christian education influences every aspect of daily life.

The philosophical underpinnings for Christian education are found in the Bible. The Bible—God's book—tells God's story. It is his truth. The Bible tells us who God is and what he has done for us. The Bible (also called *Scripture* or *God's Word*) informs everything that occurs in a Christian school, including the curriculum, the school's climate, and all social interaction. In a very personal way, the Bible speaks to the needs of every child, parent, and teacher in a Christian school population. It recognizes that all of us—parents, teachers, and students—are flawed by sin. It offers the only possible resolution for that deadly flaw—the sacrifice Jesus made to save us. As redeemed sinners, purchased with Jesus' sacrificial death, we are works in progress. Likewise, those schools and school systems that claim the name Christian are *works in progress.* The model described in this book is an ideal, a goal, something that every Christian school is striving to achieve. The Bible's central message of forgiveness and reconciliation with God is the only power that can cause a Christian school to make progress toward that goal.

The Bible binds parents and teachers together in a Christian school community. It provides the framework for their solemn partnership and serves as their mutual charter, keeping them on the same page and working together toward the same goals.

While we've been careful not to overwhelm you with quotations from the Bible, don't be surprised to find a few Scripture passages sprinkled throughout. Christians rally around God's Word. In his Word we find the inspiration, encouragement, guidance, and comfort to take on the sacred business of preparing our children for their futures.

Learning is a wonderful process. It engages the whole child on a path of physical, mental, emotional, and spiritual development. As your child is maturing, you will also be doing some growing of your own. That's a very good thing, though it won't always be easy. We hope this book will become a valuable part of your own personal learning curve. The value of a child's education improves exponentially as his or her parents grow through the same process.

While it would be easy to finish reading *Foundations* in just a few sittings, it is designed for a more studied approach. Constructed around four themes—PEACE, HOPE, JOY, and LOVE—it encourages parents and teachers to use the book in an ongoing conversation about school issues and educational concerns. In this way, the book serves as the umbrella for a complete package of materials that can be presented in a comprehensive four- or five-year program. The aim is to bring parents and teachers together around God's Word to discuss the many blessings that Christian education has to offer.

If a learning process is based on a false premise, it is possible to construct a curriculum that teaches foolish or even harmful lessons. During the Middle Ages, when the Black Plague swept through Europe and education was at one of its lowest points in the world's history, a law was passed requiring teachers to instruct their pupils to say "God bless you" whenever somebody sneezed. The law was inspired by the superstitious conviction that evil spirits were expelled from the body by sneezing.

Today the idea that sneezing expels evil spirits is ludicrous. Superstition is clearly not a solid educational foundation.

When the foundational footings for education are not sound, the rest of the structure will be vulnerable and unstable. For any educational model to have integrity, it must have a legitimate basis in truth.

The Bible's central figure is Jesus Christ. Scripture tells us that Jesus is God's truth in the flesh. From the many Bible lessons that your child will learn at a Christian school, you will become more familiar with Jesus. For now, one lesson that he taught is especially helpful when considering educational models.

> Two men each decided to build a new house. The wiser man looked for property that had a base of solid rock to provide a strong foundation. The second man wasn't so fussy. He was in a hurry. He never even considered looking for land that offered solid footing. It never occurred to him that the integrity and stability of his new house would require a sound foundation. Instead, he constructed his dream home on top of a sand dune.
>
> Sometime later a hurricane swept through the area—winds well in excess of 100 miles per hour. When it was time to survey the damage, it was discovered that the house that had been constructed on bedrock had some minor cosmetic damage, but the foundation was firm. The house remained, proudly standing right where the wise man had built it.
>
> There wasn't much left of the fool's home. Whatever the torrential winds hadn't destroyed, the tidal floods had washed away. It lacked the structural integrity to withstand the storm (Matthew 7:24-27).

Jesus was teaching a simple but profound lesson about life. If our lives are tethered firmly to the bedrock of God's Word, we will be able to withstand the dangerous storms that will inevitably sweep through our lives. Because our lives are products of the educational models that are in force as we grow, Jesus' words speak to those educational models. If you build an educational system on a foundation made of shifting sand, you can expect to reap the unhappy rewards of such a foolish choice. A wise building plan would instead establish a child's education on a foundation that has integrity, one that inspires confidence, one that is grounded in truth. This book presents an educational model intent on building human houses that have the integrity to remain standing forever.

In the early 1980s, American education awoke to a troubling new trend. At an alarming rate, spiraling school violence—a concern that had not previously been on the radar—was finding its way into our nation's classrooms. Gang violence was spilling into the corridors of our high schools. The stories children told of daily confrontations at school, sometimes involving knives or guns, caused parents to question the safety and security of the schools to which they were sending their children.

Then, on April 20, 1999, armed with semiautomatic weapons, two teens calmly walked into their local high school in Columbine, Colorado, and opened fire on their fellow students. By the time the rampage ended, the two had shot 36 of their fellow students and one teacher before turning the guns on themselves. Twenty-four of their victims survived. Thirteen did not. In the days that followed, an entire generation watched in horror as newscasts replayed footage of the tragic scene. The security of our nation's schools instantly became the number one concern for parents with school-age children.

More than a decade later, peace of mind is still parents' number one priority when choosing a school for their children. Today school systems carefully assess their vulnerability. They are busily engaged in developing vigilant and effective security plans for dealing with a variety of potentially dangerous scenarios. Curriculums now instruct young people on how to deal with bullies and help squelch school violence. Yet parents everywhere continue to express their concerns: "I want my child to attend a school that provides a safe and secure environment. I want my child to learn in a peaceful setting that is free from conflict, threats, and bullies."

PART
ONE

"Make every effort to live in peace with all men and to be holy; without holiness no one will see the Lord."

Hebrews 12:14

CHAPTER ONE

R. E. S. P. E. C. T.

It's inevitable. Walk the halls of any elementary or high school in America on the first day of classes, and you are likely to hear teachers repeating the *R-word* during their student orientations. *Respect* is a very important word in the everyday life of a school. It is a concept that applies to students, their parents, and the teachers who will have contact with the students on a daily basis. Like the air we breathe, mutual respect is one common value we all cling to. Without respect it is impossible to operate a school system, a school, or a classroom.

The Stanford Encyclopedia of Philosophy states that word experts have variously defined *respect* as a mode of behavior, a kind of valuing, a motive, an attitude, a feeling, a principle, a duty, an entitlement, a moral virtue. It matters little if the setting is a secular school, a parochial school, a private school, or a charter school—all of these definitions of *respect* apply to all school settings all of the time.

LEARNING IN A SOCIAL ENVIRONMENT

Schools are communities. They are microcosms of the larger societies in which we all must function. They are collections of people, all living in an environment that encourages engagement in some aspect of learning. The health of the fabric that holds school communities together can be measured by the relative health of the relationships of its participants. In schools, relationships will either grow and mature over time and through common experiences or they will deteriorate into dysfunction.

People who do not receive the respect of others are likely to have little respect for themselves. All who are part of the school community (students, parents, teachers, bus drivers, maintenance people, etc.) are expected to embrace the value of respecting others.

Healthy relationships are a critical component of any communal learning setting. Without exception, the need for mutual respect places a burden of responsibility on every member of the school community. Each member will need to show respect for

- *authority,*
- *parents and the parental role,*
- *teachers and the instructive role,*
- *students and their levels of understanding,*
- *safety rules,*
- *school rules,*
- *civil law,*
- *family,*
- *ethnic and cultural traditions,*
- *other people's rights and feelings,*
- *our country's flag as the symbol of a free and democratic form of government,*
- *our country's leaders,*
- *the unvarnished truth,* and
- *the right to hold differing opinions.*

WHEN SOCIETIES BREAK DOWN

In one of the early narratives in the Bible, we get to see a clear picture of what happens when the individual members of a society are completely lacking in respect for one another. In the well-known account of the great flood, we learn that God saw mankind's rampant wickedness. The people living at that time had only evil in their hearts. The Bible says, "Now the earth was corrupt in God's sight and was full of violence . . . for all the people on earth had corrupted their ways" (Genesis 6:11,12). That comment reveals a lot. Imagine an entire society in which each individual is so self-centered, so morally bankrupt, and so lacking in respect for others that all social order has completely broken down! Lawlessness ruled the day. It must have been horrible.[1] Failure to respect the law and honor the rights of others ultimately and inevitably results in chaos, violent behaviors, and bloodshed.

---

[1] A present-day comparison might be made to sections of some American cities where police no longer have much of a presence because the crime rate is too high and violence is so prevalent that to patrol has become virtually impossible.

God intervened with a terrible flood so that lawlessness would not entirely engulf his created planet and snuff mankind into extinction. But he saved eight people—Noah and his family. Every other human being died a violent death.

No school can afford to let the learning community turn from a peaceful environment into a violent, chaotic place where outlaws freely roam and threats of one kind or another drive every part of daily life. Disrespect cannot be tolerated, because it leads to behaviors that will ultimately dismantle a peaceful community.

Adults and children alike need to learn how to get along with others and have respect for one another. That is why educators make respect such a high priority, explaining from day one that everyone will be expected to demonstrate respect for everyone else.

The fundamental need for mutual respect in a school environment begins with teachers respecting their students. Educators show respect for their young students by treating everyone fairly, by valuing each and every child as a unique individual, by recognizing personal gifts and abilities that God has given to each child, and by holding high standards of respect for all human beings— regardless of ethnicity, race, religious beliefs, socioeconomic status, or political opinions. Even when we disagree, we must learn to disagree respectfully.

The relative health of the relationship between a parent and his or her child's teacher(s) is of fundamental importance. This relationship is, in theory, a partnership among equals and dedicated to the singular cause of teaching the child. Education experts are concerned that this critical relationship has been steadily eroding for several decades.

PEACE IN THE PARENT-TEACHER PARTNERSHIP

The general reminder that respect is essential among all students applies also to the parent-teacher relationship. When parents and teachers are at odds, learning suffers. The curricula (the list of subject areas that are to be taught) can vary widely. The climate can be quite different from one school to another. But the success of preschools, elementary schools, middle schools, junior highs, and high schools depends largely on the unity and strength of the partnership between educators and parents.[2] In this relationship, both parties have to be committed to honest and open communication. Their common goals require

---

[2]Some schools insist that at least one parent signs a partnership contract that clearly spells out expectations for both parents and teachers.

complete agreement. Both parents and teachers must be willing to work together in harmony so that these goals are met. ▪

DISCUSSIONS FOR CHAPTER ONE

1. List some ways in which children demonstrate disrespect for other children.

2. In practical terms, what does respect look like from a child's perspective? from a parent's perspective? from a teacher's perspective?

3. Do you see any signs of moral breakdown in your community that may have their origin in a lack of respect for others?

4. In what ways do you see yourself working closely with your partner in Christian education?

   • In what areas do you think there is some potential for conflict regarding how education should be conducted?

5. Read James 2:1-10. Why is the subject of favoritism an especially appropriate discussion point when it comes to choosing a school for your child?

   • How does this passage in the book of James lay a biblical foundation for a school system that is very careful and conscientious about not showing favoritism of any kind in its approach to education?

   • What argument does the apostle James make in verse 5 that helps us understand how God would like us to treat one another at home and at school?

CHAPTER TWO

The "I Want" Syndrome

How well do you know your child? Do you remember bringing the tiny bundle home? Infants are so vulnerable and helpless. It is difficult to imagine selfish desires lurking about in their innocent little hearts. A parent gets a glimpse of infant self-awareness only when hunger or the discomfort of a messy diaper calls for attention. A few shrill outbursts—a newborn's way of communicating urgency—and we get the message.

Did the Terrible Twos[1] alter your thinking? By age 2 most parents know their child has a will. Initially it can be a charming discovery. A two-year-old's willful demands are proof-positive that a real person is living inside that tiny body. Such stubborn self-awareness may even look and sound vaguely familiar. Parents often begin to see little hints of themselves in their child's me-first behaviors.

A CHILD'S VIEW

Childhood experts theorize that a two-year-old has occasional fits of unreasonable, willful behavior because of the child's limited vocabulary. This is a valid observation. But observant parents also know that their child's unreasonable demands reflect a self-centered worldview and a self-serving attitude. When a two-year-old shouts "I want" in every other sentence, a parent gets that this child believes the world revolves around him or her. And if the child's demands are not met, the result could be characterized as *conflict*.

So, how does a parent know all this?

The answer is that you and I each draw upon a lifetime of experience. We know what went on in our own hearts and minds when we were young. We understand the attitudes of our kids because we have attitudes of our own. We *want*—and some of our wanting is wrong. Should we be surprised then that our kids sometimes want in ways that are selfish and self-serving?

---

[1] For some children this brief life stage may come before age 2; for others it may come later.

Selfish wanting—the kind that slavishly serves our personal desires—is a spiritual affliction. We all suffer from it. Many of us may know it by another name: *sin*. And, sadly, we've passed it on to our children.

An inspired Bible author named James wrote a letter that was intended reading for every follower of Jesus. James was a brilliant student of human behavior. He understood how conflict works and what causes it. In his letter, James asked this powerful question: *"What causes fights and quarrels among you?"* (4:1). (In the question James posed, you can almost hear the voice of a teacher who has just walked in on a fight, saying, *"What's going on here?"*)

James bluntly answered his own question: "Don't [your fights and quarrels] come from your desires that battle within you? You want something but don't get it. You kill and covet, but you cannot have what you want. You quarrel and fight" (4:1,2).

Do you feel the finger of judgment pointing at you? James is taking aim at you and me. He says that *you* are the problem; *I* am the problem. The problem is that we—all of us—*want*. And sometimes *we* want wrong things, immoral things, things that lead us to sin.

James is right, of course. We are by nature selfish people. We want. And our selfish wanting sometimes leads us to sin.

Not all wanting is wrong (like wanting a decent education for our kids). Yet some of our wanting is very wrong (like wanting our neighbor's job or spouse). These same truths apply to our children. Sometimes the things children want are just plain wrong.

Most people try to avoid talking about sin. But when people intentionally avoid talking about anything, you know the subject they are avoiding is serious.

Sin is a serious matter. It leads to unending personal disaster. Sin tragically destroys the one relationship in our lives that can offer real hope for an eternal future; it trashes our relationship with our loving God.

The problem of sin has to be dealt with in every individual's life. In a Christian school, sin is dealt with on a daily basis, but not always in the way one might think.

A writer named Moses recorded the first occurrence of selfish wanting. He tells us that God had created a beautiful garden for our forbearers, Adam and Eve. They enjoyed a happiness there that you and I cannot begin to fathom.

God had said that they were not to eat of the fruit of one of the trees in their garden home. This gave them a chance to exercise their free will, making it possible for them to show that they trusted their Creator to know what was best for them.

Then Eve was tempted. The devil convinced her that the forbidden fruit was her ticket to becoming just like God. It was a lie. In spite of all that God had given to her, Eve wanted more. She wanted something she could not have. Adam followed Eve's lead when he should have been leading her away from temptation. Wanting caused Adam and Eve to disobey God's will. Their willful act of eating the forbidden fruit spoiled everything about God's perfect creation. While it happened a long time ago, you and I carry the legacy of their first sin. And we have passed it on to our children.

CHRISTIAN EDUCATION'S TWO MASTER LESSONS

In a Christian school, your child will learn the sad story of sin and the painful truth that he or she is a sinner. That is a hard truth for anyone to accept. Your child will also learn that fellow students, teachers, principals, and other adults are capable of saying and doing things that are not pleasing to God. Your child will learn that parents occasionally make choices that are shameful and anger God.

If sin were the only truth a Christian school had to teach, it would be a miserable place to send your child. But it isn't. Christian education is not only about sin. Christian education is based on an even greater truth that deals positively with the very negative problem of sin, and this truth does so in the most extraordinary way. We will consider this profound Bible teaching in the next chapter. ▓

DISCUSSIONS FOR CHAPTER TWO

1. Describe some ways in which your child exercises his or her own will.

2. List some ways in which you can already tell that your child is *a chip off the old block.*

3. Why is it so important for everyone in a school population to remember that teachers, parents, and students are sometimes driven by sinful desires?

4. Explain why sin is such a devastating part of the human experience.

- In what ways do you see sin doing its damage in your family?

- In what ways do you see sin doing damage in the school setting?

5. Read Matthew 25:31-46. According to Jesus' parable of the sheep and the goats, how is unbelief connected with selfishness and self-centeredness?

- How does the way we treat one another, either in the home setting or in the school setting, reflect on our relationships with Jesus?

- As a result of this little study of Jesus' parable of the sheep and the goats, what lesson do you want your child to learn both at home and in school?

CHAPTER THREE

God's Rainbow of Peace

If schoolhouse walls could talk, what memories they would share! In a perfect world, childhood would be the best of times and classroom memories would be happy thoughts. Unfortunately, we know that's not always the way it is in reality. Some classroom experiences bring heartache and sadness.

Christian schools are no different from other schools in this regard. Sometimes bad things happen. Only a naive parent would believe that jealousy, injustice, disrespect, bullying, or a host of other wrongs could never occur at a Christian school. Furthermore, honest parents understand that their own child is also capable of behaving in unloving ways toward others.

Many of the naughty things children say and do seem relatively harmless to adults. We tend to see children's sins as inconsequential. In fact, such behaviors expose the taint of the original sin that Adam and Eve passed on to every generation that followed them. The simple truth is that sin is never inconsequential.

OUR PROBLEM WITH GOD

The Bible tells us that one of God's most spectacular character traits is his absolute holiness. God never lies or deceives. His sense of justice is absolutely flawless. He carries out his perfect justice with perfect judgment. He never makes a promise only to later break it. He loves perfectly, communicates perfectly, relates perfectly. God is righteous in every way. Who would want to live under the rule and direction of an imperfect god?

But for sinners, God's holiness is a problem. He despises sin. He has declared that every sin must be punished. Our sin makes it impossible for us to live in God's presence; our imperfection separates us from our perfect Creator. To God, there is no such thing as a *little white lie,* an accidental curse, or harmless gossip. Dishonesty, hateful language, and telling lies about others are sins. To God, meanness is inexcusable. So is cheating, stealing, or defying authority. God holds each individual accountable to his perfect standard. His justice demands punishment for every thought, word, or deed that is contrary to his perfect will.

God condemns the sins that our children commit. He expects our offspring to conduct themselves perfectly. And when they don't, he applies the same moral standards to their seemingly harmless sins as he does to the most heinous adult crimes. And he is right when he does that, because he understands perfectly what sin is.

OUR ONLY HOPE

God, whom the Bible reveals as a perfectly just God, is also described as a God of boundless love. God's love dominates his divine being. His very essence is love. He loves the people who populate the world he created. He loves your child. He loves you and me personally. And he has gone to extreme lengths to overcome the obstacle of sin that separates us from his love.

When Adam and Eve sinned, their rebellion drove a wedge between them and their loving Creator. They deserved to be banished from his presence. They deserved to wallow in excruciating regret for their willful disobedience. And God did drive them out of the garden he had made for them in Eden. But he did not drive them out of his sight. Nor did he abandon them to an eternity of hellish guilt. In love, God graciously provided a solution that would justly punish sin, yet he also made a way for sinners to escape sin's eternal consequence. God promised to send a Savior—One who would be worthy of his high standard of excellence (absolute perfection to match God's own holiness). With that promise, Adam and Eve could rest assured that one day they would once again stand in their Maker's presence as pure and holy as the day he created them.

That same promise is also our legacy and our children's. That very same Bible truth is the bedrock for the unique educational model that we call *Christian education*. In a Christian school, your child will hear this amazing good news repeated again and again. It's the good news given voice in a favorite children's hymn:

> *Jesus loves me, this I know,*
> *For the Bible tells me so.*
> *Little ones to him belong;*
> *They are weak, but he is strong.*
> *Yes, Jesus loves me!*
> *Yes, Jesus loves me!*
> *Yes, Jesus loves me!*
> *The Bible tells me so.*

As God intervened in a violence-filled world, using a great flood to cleanse the earth, so he also intervened in the case of eight faithful believers. He sealed Noah, Noah's wife, Noah's three sons, and their wives into a watertight ark of his own design. These eight survived. When the floodwaters subsided, a fresh new world awaited. Through Noah and his offspring, God kept alive the hope of a promised Savior from sin. But one might be prompted to ask what Noah and the other members of his family had done to earn God's favor.

Noah and the members of his family were just as much a part of the human race as you and I. Their selfish, me-first attitude, which is so characteristic of a sinful heart, was passed on to them by their ancestors. And like us, they sinned daily. Not one of them deserved to be saved. But one thing distinguished Noah and his family from the rest of the earth's doomed population. These eight believed God when he said he would destroy the world, and they turned to God for help. They alone trusted in God's promise to send a Savior from sin. They knew God loved them and would rescue them. And because of their faith in God's promises, they were at peace with him. So, God placed a rainbow in the heavens to remind future generations that peace with him would always be tied to his promise to send a Savior.

Christian education is the only educational model that deals effectively with the sins of children, parents, and teachers. A Christian school is not free from the heartache or tears that sin causes, but God's full and free forgiveness provides a powerful way of dealing with wrongdoing. His solution to our problem with sin gives us blessings that have huge implications for our children and us in the eternal future. Talking about the peace that comes with complete forgiveness is a very high priority in the Christian school environment. And, while there are exceptions, the ongoing conversation about God's forgiveness generally translates into God-pleasing attitudes, actions, and behaviors. Gratitude for a life of true peace changes the way we think and act. ▪

DISCUSSIONS FOR CHAPTER THREE

1. Are your school-year memories happy memories or unhappy memories? Explain.

2. Give an example of how forgiveness might be offered in an unconditional way. Then describe some conditions that people might try to attach to their offers of forgiveness.

3. If we offer conditional forgiveness to someone, is it really forgiveness? Explain.

4. Explain why God must punish sin. Then explain how God dealt with sin in a way that would leave sinners completely free of all guilt.

5. What saved Noah and his family from drowning in the great flood?

- What saves you and your family from certain destruction in hell?

6. Read Romans 6:23. Why is it so important to talk with our children about sin and its eternal consequences?

- Why are we tempted to downplay the importance of sin in our lives?

- How does this text in Romans take us from the absolute hopelessness of sin to the total hopefulness of God's grace?

- After studying this verse, what lesson do you want your child to learn both at home and at school?

CHAPTER FOUR

The Peacemaker's *Peacemaker*

Parents want their children to become mature, peace-loving citizens. In practical terms, however, *peacemaking* does not come naturally to children. If you need proof, observe them at play. The things they say and do frequently lead to conflict. This is one reason why teachers are needed; someone has to maintain order. To become *peacemakers*, children need mature adults to motivate and guide them.

Christian motivation begins at the foot of a cross. In the Christian education model, God's forgiveness motivates appropriate, peace-loving behavior.

THE MEANING OF THE CROSS

In ancient times the cross was an instrument of torture that inevitably led to a violent and painful death. Today it is the best known of all Christian symbols. Christian churches and schools display crosses in prominent places as reminders of the sacrifice Jesus made on a cross two thousand years ago outside of Jerusalem. There, on a cross outside the city walls, God's plan to save the world from the curse of sin culminated in a real historical event that changed everything. The cross is a spiritual place where sinners go for healing and renewal.

Any child can draw a cross. It consists of two intersecting perpendicular lines. The vertical line helps us visualize God's love flowing down from heaven as he reaches down to us with pardon and mercy.

On some pictured versions of the cross (called a *crucifix*), a man hangs suspended between earth and heaven. He is a human bridge between God and sinful mankind. The man is in agony. Though he is innocent, he is dying. He is dying for you, for me, for our children and grandchildren, for a world full of sinners like us. He volunteered to take on the punishment we deserve for the sins we've committed. The man's name is *Jesus*. The Bible calls him *the Christ*—the Anointed One, the Messiah—whom God promised to send. This God-man named Jesus would do the work of a Savior. When his work was finished, everything that God required of us to bring us back into his heavenly family had been completed. Nothing was left undone. Not even the smallest detail. Nothing more is required of us in order to find peace with God.

The work Christ Jesus did on our behalf has major implications for the peace we seek with one another. God wants us to live in peace with one another. He wants this peace for us because it is for our good. Through commitment, hard work, and personal sacrifice, earthly peace can sustain vibrant, healthy relationships between brothers and sisters, parents and children, friends and acquaintances, classmates and teachers. But God also wants us to remember that such temporal peace (peace that is restricted only to this life on earth) is eclipsed by the spiritual peace Christ came to bring.

From the beginning it has always been God's desire to envelope mankind in his loving peace. Yet the only world we have ever known is a world of struggle and tension, conflict and war, hatred and strife. It is impossible for human beings to accurately imagine a time when the entire created universe was wrapped in unflawed tranquility.

For Adam and Eve, God's garden paradise was filled to overflowing with a satisfying and harmonious intimacy with their Creator. The profound peace of their conflict-*less* existence made such an idyllic life possible. They lived in unimaginable security.

Then their peace was shattered by sin. Suddenly conflict became an integral part of the human experience. And life on our planet grew tenuous.

After the fall, the promise that God had given to Adam and Eve echoed down through the long centuries as God's people waited for it to be fulfilled. More than two thousand years later, the planet that greeted God's Prince of peace (Jesus) was eerily nestled in a span of history that is still remembered as the *Pax Romana* (the "Roman Peace"). Ironically, this brief global hiatus from war was stitched together with violence and brutality. In human flesh, God's Son was no stranger to conflict, even as a newborn baby. The shepherds still remembered the angels' song celebrating *peace on earth*, even as Mary and Joseph were fleeing to Egypt with their small child to escape the murderous hand of Herod.[1]

It was a pensive adult Jesus who bluntly observed, "In this world you will have trouble." His words are as relevant today as they were when he said them. Thankfully, he added, "I have told you these things, so that in me you may have peace. . . . Take heart! I have overcome the world" (John 16:33).

---

[1] You can read the grim account in Matthew 2:1-23.

Overcoming the world meant that Christ willingly exposed himself to the lies of unbelievers. Jesus faced the unjust judgments of evil men, suffered the ridicule of thugs, and endured a cruel and painful execution. He knew what it was to be hated. When we think of the anguish and injustice he suffered at the hands of sinners like us, our hearts break. But we are also deeply grateful. Where you and I deserve to be cast out of God's loving presence and thrown into the furnace of everlasting war, his Son willingly stepped forward as our substitute. He paid the price we deserved to pay. We call this his work of redemption. And because of Jesus' redemptive work, we can look forward to the eternal peace that awaits us in heaven's glory.

In a miracle that we cannot fully understand, Jesus Christ is both God and man. His mission on earth was to live the perfect life that no sinner is able to live. Moreover, he would die the punishment that sinners justly deserve. He carried the guilt of all mankind. Therefore, our eternal judge has declared us *not guilty*. Anyone who believes in Jesus will have eternal life. All of this is captured in that single vertical line of the cross, which reconnects us to our loving Creator-Father.

CHRIST AT THE CENTER

Jesus Christ—the peacemaker's Peacemaker—is at the epicenter of a Christian school. The Christmas story tells us how God sent his Son, Jesus, into our world to be born in a humble cattle shed. It is one of the highlights of the Christian calendar. Your child will hear the story of Jesus' birth in Bethlehem, learn about the angel's song that speaks about *peace on earth*, and sing songs that honor and praise his saving name. Your child will learn to pray to Jesus because he is in perfect unity with his heavenly Father. Jesus Christ is God. He deserves our worship. His cross, and the forgiveness it brings to us, moves us to live lives that are consistent with God's will.

The true story about Jesus and his loving sacrifice for sinners is sometimes called *the gospel. Gospel* means "good news." The gospel is the best news anyone could ever hope for. It tells us we are heaven-bound, and so are our children.

THE CROSSBEAM

With the vertical beam firmly anchored in the rocky scrabble at its base, we turn our attention to the cross' horizontal beam. This beam reminds us of how the Savior stretched out his arms to embrace all humanity in his own death. This picture helps us understand our relationships with the people who populate our lives.

Jesus' cross changes us. Washed clean in the blood he shed for us on the cross, we now begin to resemble our Savior. We are ready to serve others instead of being served. We love others, forgive others, help others. We share Jesus with others. The man of the cross now influences everything we say and do.

Our children's hearts will change in the same way when Christ's cross is at work in their young lives. They will learn how to reach out to others with compassion and do the work that God has prepared for them to do. Jesus' love will motivate them to behave as God wants his children to behave. They will never achieve perfection in this life, but his cross moves them to pursue life in a way that will make their parents and teachers happy and give glory to God's name.

The horizontal beam extends beyond family and friends to the broken relationships we have with those people whom we consider to be our enemies. (We will talk more about how your child will be taught to deal with personal enemies in the next chapter.) Christianity is about the kind of love that drove Christ to the cross. He died there, even for his enemies.

Christian schools teach this wonderful good news because it is the heart of the Christian faith, the heart of God's Word, and the heart of our loving God, who would do anything for the creatures he loves. None of this is embedded in the curriculum of secular schools. There, by design and prohibited by law, it is not taught and rarely practiced.

It won't always be easy to reject the world's views. It's a challenge—a test that God places before all Christian parents. God wants us to understand the difference between the way things work in his kingdom and the way they work in the various kingdoms that mankind has constructed. He wants us to wrestle with him for the help and strength we need. He wants us to apply the principles taught in his Word to our own lives and to train our own children to live according to biblical principles. With new hearts fashioned in the likeness of the Savior's heart and guided by the Holy Spirit, we will pass the test. ▪

DISCUSSIONS FOR CHAPTER FOUR

1. Do you have a cross on display somewhere in your home? (If so, what significance does it have in the lives of family members?)

2. What is meant by the statement, "The cross is a spiritual place where sinners go for healing and renewal"?

3. By far the most important result of the cross is the restored relationship between God and humans. But the cross also plays a key role in our relationships with others. What are some of the causes for conflict in a school setting?

- What are some of the causes for conflict at home?

- Why is it a good idea for either a parent or a teacher to take children aside to deal with personal conflicts privately?

- In what ways are the roles of the parent and teacher almost identical when dealing with conflict, either at home or in the school?

4. Read Colossians 1:15-22. To whom is the "He" in verse 15 referring?

- According to this text, what demonstrates that the man who went to the cross is the Son of God?

- How does the man of the cross change our lives?

- After studying this text, what important lesson do you want your child to learn at home and at school?

CHAPTER FIVE

The Battle Inside

In general, parents rank *learning to live a moral life* among the highest of all educational objectives. This is true even for those who do not profess to be a part of any organized religion. The learning curve for this particular growth objective can be severe.

It isn't easy to turn the other cheek when someone attacks you and all your friends are waiting to see what you're going to do about it. It isn't easy when a group invites you to join them, yet your conscience tells you that what they are doing is wrong. It isn't easy when you've been unfairly treated and your instinct says it's your turn to even the score. Being a child of God isn't easy. Nor will it be easy for you to be a patient parent when these things happen to your child.

THE *OLD ADAM* WITHIN

As God's children, we want to do the right thing—the God-pleasing thing. But that can trigger an internal struggle, pitting the new person we've become as followers of Christ (sometimes called the *new Man in Christ*) against the old sin-driven person within us. Martin Luther called that nasty, natural, self-serving, former self our old Adam. He said that each day, with God's help, we should drown the old Adam within. That is violent language. It demonstrates how important it is to keep driving sin out of our lives. If we don't deal firmly with our old Adam, that old man in us could still gain the upper hand and cause us to lose our faith.

God has promised to help us overcome our old Adam. And he has promised to help our children in the same way.

One key resource that God gives for this ongoing internal battle is the Ten Commandments. Earlier we said that the Ten Commandments convict us of wrongdoing. They act like a mirror. The person staring back at us is riddled with sin—damaged goods in God's holy eyes, so badly flawed that God could not possibly allow such a vile offender into his throne room.

God's mirror doesn't lie. It tells us how desperately we need his mercy. It reminds us that we must depend on him for help in undoing the things we've done (or not done) to disappoint him. When God's children are convicted by his law, they are sorry (The technical word is *contrite.*) for wrong behavior. They repent and confess their sin.

Their repentance is not an emotion but a motion—a constant moving away from a life of disobedience and sin toward a life that is dedicated to Christ and lived as his disciple. To repent is not merely to *feel bad* but to confess that I am bad through and through by virtue of my sinful nature. I am a lawbreaker, who fears, loves, and trusts other gods above the God who created me, loves me, and died to save me. God's forgiveness is already waiting. He gives to our children and us the peace we need, reassuring us that all of our sins are forgiven for Jesus' sake. It is the good news that every human soul longs for—the gospel light that pours life into a hopelessly dead sinner.

A NEW PERSON EMERGES

There is another application of these same Ten Commandments. As God's children we are eager to learn how he wants us to live our lives, not to earn his favor but to show our gratitude for all that he has done for us. We need a standard, a measuring stick, to help us know how he wants us to behave rightly and to help us understand what wrong-headed thoughts, words, and actions we should avoid in order to please him.

The Ten Commandments serve as God's standard for living the moral life. Here's a summary:

1. *Do not worship false idols.*

2. *Honor and respect God's holy name.*

3. *Keep the Sabbath Day holy.*

4. *Honor your father and mother and all who have been placed in authority over you.*

5. *Do not hurt or kill your neighbor.*

6. *Do not commit adultery.*

7. *Do not steal.*

8. *Do not speak falsely about others.*

9. *Do not desire your neighbor's spouse.*

10. *Don't covet any of your neighbor's possessions.*

If it were possible for us to keep all of God's Ten Commandments perfectly, heaven would be ours by virtue of our own holy actions, words, and thoughts. But that isn't going to happen. We are sinners. We were born sinners. In this life we are going to be faced with decisions about doing right and wrong. The same battle is going on inside every man, woman, and child who follows Jesus. God's people want to make right choices—choices that will please God. So often we don't. And we want to avoid those wrong-headed decisions that will anger and disappoint him. But so often we fail. Our children are experiencing this daily. Their internal struggle is a constant part of living the Christian life. Anyone who believes that he or she can win this struggle without God's help is a fool.

WRESTLING WITH GOD

A Bible narrative about a man named Jacob illustrates God's desire to bless us with powerful resources for fighting our internal battles. Jacob was no stranger to conflict. His older brother, Esau, had vowed to kill him after Jacob had wrongfully walked off with Esau's birthright. For 20 years Jacob lived beyond Esau's reach. But Jacob always knew that one day he would return home to face his brother's wrath.

As the storyline develops, it looks as though the brothers would finally meet in mortal combat. Jacob's entourage was neither prepared nor equipped for battle. So Jacob shrewdly divided his caravan into two groups and sent emissaries ahead with lavish gifts to placate his brother.

Then, on the eve of what was shaping up to be a face-off to the death, Jacob was alone, deep in prayer. A stranger appeared. Jacob recognized the stranger as the Lord God himself, so he boldly demanded a blessing.

The stranger engaged Jacob in an intense hand-to-hand struggle that lasted throughout the night. As the battle raged, the stranger's embrace actually strengthened Jacob and encouraged him to fight on. At dawn the stranger finally relented, but not before leaving Jacob with a hip injury to remind him of the Lord's endless love. Then the stranger announced the blessing that Jacob had been pleading for—and a new name: *Israel*. It means "one who wrestles with God."

In faith you and I bear the same identity as Jacob. Each of us is a one-who-wrestles-with-God. Each of our children is a little one-who-wrestles-with-God. Like every other child in a Christian school, your child will wrestle with God on a daily basis—at school, on the playground, in transit, at home. Though these struggles may involve pain, they will never be driven by hatred or enmity. God uses these battles as a platform for demonstrating his astounding love. He wants nothing more than to bless you (and your child) with every resource needed to carry on the good fight of faith.

God brings the fight to us, not to destroy us but to reach out with his blessings of hope. He brings the fight to us to help us remember that we are not alone in our daily battles with our spiritual enemies. Without these blessings we have no hope for overcoming our conflicts or conquering the sins associated with them. With God's blessings we are intrepid warriors; we cannot be defeated. God wants us to be persistent in seeking his powerful gifts and to remember that he is the source for all of our blessings. Our loving God engages us in these intimate and personal wrestling matches to remind us that he will provide everything we need for our fight against the old Adam. ■

DISCUSSIONS FOR CHAPTER FIVE

1. Share some of the wrestling matches that you have fought with God because he has blessed you with a child to raise.

- How have you been blessed by these wrestling matches with God?

2. Why is it such a serious mistake to believe that we can do battle with our enemies—the devil, the world, and our own sinful flesh—without God's help?

3. List some of the blessings or benefits we have as a result of our daily wrestling matches with God.

4. Make a list of spiritual resources that God gives us to fight the good fight of faith.

5. Read Ezekiel 11:19. What surgical procedure in modern medicine are you reminded of when you read this text that describes what happens when an unbeliever comes to faith in Jesus?

- Read Romans 6:3,4. How does the apostle Paul describe the same transformation?

- Read Romans 7:5,6. What happens to our behaviors when this transformation process occurs?

- Read Psalm 3. According to this psalm of David, how does God want us to approach our battles with the enemies of our souls?

- After studying these texts, what important lesson do you want your child to learn at home and at school?

CHAPTER SIX

Peace by Rule of Law

Learning suffers when children do not feel secure in their environment. A hostile school climate teaches learners to be afraid and anxious. Conversely, when classroom rules and school policies are reasonable, fair, and consistently enforced, they suppress chaos and keep conflict in check.

In this chapter we will turn our attention to still another use of God's law. This application of divine law applies to everyone and promotes a secure and peaceful environment.

THE LAW AS A CURB

Though everything about God's creation was once absolutely perfect, nothing in our world today is flawless. Sin is everywhere. And so are the awful consequences of sin. Sin poisons our relationships. It corrupts society and corrodes our surroundings. We see it in our own lives and in the lives of the people dearest to us, including our own children.

Nothing good has ever come from sin. And if sin were to have its way in our world, as it apparently had among the people of Noah's day, our planet would become so corrupt and violent that mankind would quickly destroy it all and ruin any chances for God to reach out to sinners with his plan of salvation. This is one very good reason why lawbreaking cannot be tolerated.

Sometimes God's law functions like a street curb. A curb's purpose is to keep traffic on the street, where it belongs. The law restrains us. And though it doesn't curtail all sin, it does keep sin from running roughshod over our civilization and plunging us into utter chaos and darkness. In the microcosm of a school, one function of the law is to control outbreaks of sinful behavior that could lead to anarchy and bedlam.

The authority from which the law proceeds comes from the holy and eternal Lawgiver. The Ten Commandments summarize God's will for all people. And one of those commandments—the Fourth—summarily treats the matter of human authority.

THE FOURTH COMMANDMENT AND HONORING AUTHORITY

The Fourth Commandment is the first commandment that pertains to our relationships with one another. It introduces the entire set of seven of God's commandments (the Fourth through the Tenth) that govern interaction among people (the cross' horizontal beam). In the Fourth Commandment, God says, "Honor your father and your mother, so that you may live long in the land the LORD your God is giving you" (Exodus 20:12).

As adults, you and I honor our parents by living wholesome lives and passing their values on to our children and grandchildren. Even if one's father or mother did a poor job of parenting and lacked strong moral convictions, the principle still stands. God wants us to hold the parental role in very high esteem. He wants us to submit to authority in general and in principle.

God places some awesome responsibilities on a father and mother when he blesses them with children. Parenting is one of the most difficult of all human endeavors. It is especially difficult in a culture as complex and open as ours. As parents, we hold the futures of our progeny in our own decision-making power. With such responsibility, God has also given us the authority to oversee our children's progress and to make wise decisions with regard to their upbringing.

By extension, some of the authority that God gives to parents also applies to other individuals. People who guard and protect us and our children in other segments of society also have authority. Christian educators, for example, have been given authority over those children whose parents have placed them into their care. Similarly, God has blessed us with civic agencies, lawmakers, and individuals who have the God-given authority to govern. Because this authority comes from God, we are to honor it implicitly. Moreover, as part of our parental responsibility, we train our children to honor and respect those whom God has placed into positions of authority over them.

The Christian education model teaches that parental authority is given by divine mandate and that, by extension, there are other representatives of God's authority on earth whose offices deserve our honor and respect. The principle applies even when public officials fail to govern in a God-pleasing way.

The Bible provides a number of texts that teach this principle. In Matthew 22:21 the Bible says that Jesus told church leaders to "give to Caesar what is Caesar's, and to God what is God's." Jesus said this, knowing that Caesar was a brutal leader and a pagan.

Jesus' followers didn't always agree. They were not able to recognize that God could still use Caesar's corrupt government to produce positive benefits. But that is exactly what happened. The peace ushered in by brutal Roman rule enabled the good news of Jesus to spread quickly throughout the civilized world.

After all is said and done, God still remains in charge of all things. He governs the universe he created. He does this through people to whom he grants temporary and limited authority to govern as his human representatives. Individuals with such God-given authority may also be empowered to establish rules, regulations, laws, and policies.

Man-made laws frequently reflect the intent of God's Ten Commandments. To illustrate, it is not uncommon for schools to note that cheating breaks a school rule. Cheating is a form of stealing, because it robs another student of the answers he or she has worked hard to learn. The Seventh Commandment addresses cheating indirectly when it says, "You shall not steal."

HUMAN LAWS, RULES, AND POLICIES VERSUS GOD'S LAW

Some human rules and laws have no direct connection with God's Word or the Ten Commandments. A school might, as a matter of school policy, require a signed permission slip from each child who wishes to participate in a field trip. But God's Word doesn't discuss field trips or permission slips. The rule just makes good sense in the light of those civil laws that make teachers responsible for the safety of the children in their care.

Other man-made regulations and laws may be open to discussion when God's Word has neither commanded nor forbidden certain activities. Mr. and Mrs. Jones have a family rule that says their children will be in bed by eight o'clock on all school nights. And they enforce it. Nothing in the Bible suggests a bedtime for children. But the parental authority that God has given to Mr. and Mrs. Jones gives them the prerogative to set such a rule, and they make sure their children abide by it.

Mr. and Mrs. Smith, on the other hand, don't mind if their children stay up well beyond 10 o'clock. They likewise have a God-given prerogative to set up their own house rules. They have reasoned that their children need to learn to exercise some discretion for making wise bedtime choices. In both cases God leaves it up to wise parents to make thoughtful choices. When parents exercise responsibility with integrity, they give glory to God by using their sanctified will.

God does not give either the Joneses or the Smiths the right to judge each other, though their choices are very different. Jesus doesn't want us judging one another in such matters.

In a school setting, the individual choices we make regarding issues that do not directly fall within the boundaries of God's Ten Commandments can cause friction between parents and teachers, and between parents and other parents. At such times it is important to remember that, as Jesus' followers, our first priority is to demonstrate Christlike love for others. When we disagree about things that God has not directly spoken about in his Word, we may need to wrestle with him, asking for help to find a course that humbly expresses our love and acknowledges another individual's right to hold a view that is contrary to our own. ■

DISCUSSIONS FOR CHAPTER SIX

1. List some of the awesome responsibilities that God has given you by virtue of your role as a parent or as a Christian educator.

2. How can a parent or teacher determine if a child who has sinned should be approached with God's law or the sweet gospel message of forgiveness?

   • Why is this decision such an important consideration in disciplinary matters?

3. When disciplining, how should a parent or teacher decide if it is best to apply God's law as a mirror, as a guide, or as a curb?

4. Make a list of parental choices for which God gives parents the freedom to make wise, sanctified decisions on behalf of their children.

   • Give some examples of how parents could misapply this freedom.

5. Read Romans 13:1-5. What principle is the apostle Paul laying down in this text that applies to the home, the school, the workplace, and society in general?

- As a result of your study of this text, what lesson do you want your child to learn at home and in school?

CHAPTER SEVEN

Little Peacemakers

Conflict has a way of surrounding us and our children with temptation. That is why it is so important to learn how to resolve it. In this chapter we will examine seven Bible principles to disarm conflict at home or school.

Knowing when to flee and when to aggressively stand one's ground can be a difficult decision for kids. In his wisdom, God chose not to provide a simple formula for addressing this dilemma. While the Bible clearly teaches us to run away from temptation, running away from a fight is not the same as fleeing from sin.[1] There are times when we may have to take a stand for a just cause.

Some parents teach their children to stand firm in the face of aggression. Others place their emphasis on running away from a fight. Neither approach is right or wrong. But there is a better way of teaching kids how to make these difficult choices without locking them into a programmed response.

Wise parents and teachers look for opportunities to discuss conflict and conflict-resolution strategies with children. Kids need to know, for example, what bullying behaviors look like and why they are so dangerous. It is helpful to walk children through hypothetical scenarios so that they will know when it is appropriate to stand up to a tyrant. They need someone to explain that telling a parent or teacher about bullying activity is not the same thing as being cowardly or vindictive.

THE *DON'T-LET-THE-SUN-SET-ON-YOUR-ANGER* PRINCIPLE

When someone wrongs us, anger is a common response. Unbridled anger can, and often does, turn into hatred. Hatred is a dark place in the human

---

[1] Conflict has many faces. Some conflicts are manifested in flailing fists, while other conflicts involve icy stares or mean-spirited words. When we use the word *fight*, its meaning encompasses all situations in which people demonstrate a potential for hating others.

psyche. To hate someone is to wish them ill. It destroys relationships and eliminates any hope for showing love or compassion.

The Bible tells us there is urgency to resolving disputes. We are to do so sooner rather than later so that our anger cannot degenerate into hatred. God wants us to take the initiative in restoring peace to a relationship that has soured. Jesus said, "If you are offering your gift at the altar and there remember that your brother has something against you, leave your gift there in front of the altar. First go and be reconciled to your brother; then come and offer your gift" (Matthew 5:23,24). Children should learn to make every effort to sort things out in a damaged relationship, even when they may not have caused the conflict. They should be encouraged to immediately seek a resolution to the conflict.

THE *PLANK-IN-YOUR-EYE* PRINCIPLE

Some children delight in finding fault with others and correcting them. By age 2 most children know that finger pointing can put others in an unfavorable light. To a child, and sadly to many adults as well, putting others in an unfavorable light often means more favorable light for *me* (more evidence of our sinful inclination to pander to self).

Jesus said, "Why do you look at the speck of sawdust in your brother's eye and pay no attention to the plank in your own eye? How can you say to your brother, 'Let me take the speck out of your eye,' when all the time there is a plank in your own eye? You hypocrite, first take the plank out of your own eye, and then you will see clearly to remove the speck from your brother's eye" (Matthew 7:3-5).

Jesus' *Plank-in-Your-Eye* principle is a sobering reminder to deal first with the sin that lurks in our own hearts and lives. Only then will we have the right attitude for helping others deal with their sinful behaviors.

Kids would like to believe they never do anything wrong. Their young consciences have a hard time acknowledging the truth about the dark thoughts that contaminate their hearts. (Sound familiar?) Parents and teachers can help children remove the planks in their eyes by holding them accountable for the wrong things they say and do. We can reinforce this concept by expecting children to verbally acknowledge their sins. A simple *I'm sorry* makes the point. When a child is contrite because the law has done its work, the heartwarming message that Jesus died to remove all of our guilt (the gospel) is the most positive and encouraging reinforcement anyone can hear.

Taking the plank out of my own eye is a humbling process—one that places me at the foot of Jesus' cross. Moms, dads, and Christian teachers are always looking for opportunities to offer themselves as humble examples of how to deal with the planks lodged in their own eyes.

THE *IF-YOUR-BROTHER-SINS-AGAINST-YOU* PRINCIPLE

Most children understand how it feels to have a brother, a sister, or a classmate say or do something that is intended to hurt. Jesus' plan for dealing with someone who has hurt me seems like a no-brainer for parents and Christian educators to teach to children. The steps found in Matthew chapter 18 are clear:

1. *"Go and show him his fault, just between the two of you" (verse 15).*

2. *"If he will not listen, take one or two others along, so that 'every matter may be established by the testimony of two or three witnesses'" (verse 16).*

3. *"If he refuses to listen to them, tell it to the church" (verse 17). (For a child, the "church" is the teacher or parent who serves as God's earthly representative.) And,*

4. *"If he refuses to listen even to the church, treat him as you would a pagan or a tax collector" (verse 17).*

But as simple as this strategy may seem, there is great danger in training children to follow the steps of Jesus' plan if we forget to include the most critical element.

The critical element is the loving concern that served as Jesus' underlying premise for sharing his plan with us in the first place. (Read all of Matthew chapter 18, especially Jesus' parable about a shepherd leaving his flock of 99 sheep to go after 1 that had gotten lost.) By following Jesus' plan, yet ignoring the purpose for this loving process aimed at restoring a sinner to God's heavenly fold, we turn a gospel-driven concern for sinners into a law-driven distortion of God's intent. Doing that actually teaches kids to judge others.

Christian education teaches both *the plan* and *the purpose* for using Jesus' four-step plan. Christian education reminds children that when they are tempted to point out the sins of others, they must first look into their own hearts to uncover the motive behind their accusation. If the motive is to get revenge or to serve their own selfish interests, they are following Jesus' plan for a very wrong reason.

THE *SEVEN-TIMES-SEVEN* PRINCIPLE

If you've spent time with children, you've probably caught yourself saying, "How many times do I have to tell you to . . . ?" Then you suddenly realized that no matter how you completed the sentence, it would sound hollow and worn-out because you had said the same thing so many times before.

Each child is a *chip off the old block*. How often don't you and I appear before our eternal judge with a plea for mercy after committing the same old sin for the umpteenth time? God's loving response is always the same: "You're forgiven because my Son died to pay for that sin. Now don't do it anymore." With God there is no limit to the number of times that he will forgive us, even if it is for sins we have repeated over and over.

One of Jesus' disciples, a fellow whom Jesus had named Peter, struggled with this same question: "How often do I have to forgive someone who keeps on offending me?" he asked. "Would seven times be a good hypothetical limit?"

Jesus suggested a different hypothetical number, one that would not be easy to keep track of. "Forgive him 49 times," said Jesus, "or 490 times." He meant that it is better still if we don't keep track. There is no ceiling on forgiveness. Following Jesus means that we will not attach conditions to our forgiveness when others sin against us.

THE *FORGIVE-AND-FORGET* PRINCIPLE

Children can be great manipulators. One technique kids learn early in life is to attach riders (or *conditions*) to their forgiveness as a way of leveraging their own agendas. Sometimes it is not enough to teach a child to say, "I forgive you." For some it may be necessary to add the words, "I've also *forgotten* what you did to me."[2]

Peacemaker Ministries has developed a simple, four-part promise to help people let go of the sins that others have committed against them.

I will not dwell on this incident.

I will not bring this incident up again to use it against you.

I will not talk to others about this incident.

---

[2]In a sinless, perfect world, we would never have to try to intentionally forget what someone has done to hurt us. But in a sinful world, failing to be able to completely forget an offense is not the sin. The sin is nursing the grudge, seeking to gain leverage by allowing someone else's sins to hang above that person's head so that the sword of your judgment is ready to fall at your command.

I will not let this incident stand between us or hinder our relationship.
(From *The Peacemaker: A Biblical Guide to Resolving Personal Conflict* by Ken Sande.)

THE *TURN-THE-OTHER-CHEEK* PRINCIPLE

One of the Bible's most difficult teachings is a lesson about getting revenge. Not only does Jesus tell us that we are to resist the temptation to even the score, he also tells us that we are to demonstrate our love for the person who has just hit us. In fact, he tells us to pray for that person. In the heat of conflict, that's a high ideal to follow. Even mature Christians struggle with it.

When someone punches us in the face or hurts us with words that cut, the world's response is predictable: strike back, if for no other reason than as a deterrent. Make sure your enemy knows you will not stand still for getting hit again.

Jesus teaches us to turn the other cheek. And he backs up this approach with his own living example.

How easy it would have been for the Son of God to retaliate against the people who spit at him, drove thorns into his skull, and nailed him to a cross! Instead, he prayed for them, "Father, forgive them, for they do not know what they are doing" (Luke 23:34). He turned the other cheek for us and for those who were unjustly executing him. Imagine what our eternal futures would have been like if he had decided instead to take revenge!

The *Turn-the-Other-Cheek* principle is a hard teaching because it forces children to recognize that their faith in Jesus is also a call to stand tall in the face of ridicule or danger. This teaching stands in stark contrast with the way the world would have us respond. Initially, children see Jesus' teaching as an unfair proposition; it just doesn't make sense. Their response provides a great opportunity to talk about the injustice of Jesus' death on Calvary's cross. He didn't deserve to be treated that way. But he willingly accepted it because he loves us. Christianity is a radical call to self-sacrifice, even as Jesus sacrificed everything for us.

From the world's perspective, someone who is treating you with such disdain deserves your hatred. Our culture reinforces this strike-back instinct. Some parents even train their children to teach the enemy a lesson he'll never forget. God does not want us seeking revenge. He has promised to punish the ungodly himself.

THE *DON'T-JUDGE-OTHERS* PRINCIPLE

In a child's world, the realities of life set in much earlier than most parents would like. At a very early age, children have already begun to observe how unfair life can be. Even the simplest games have rules. Children know that it's not fair if someone wins because he or she has cheated. Nor is it fair if a referee, an umpire, a field judge, or a parent has made a bad call. Most kids will tell you that if they could be the ref, their calls would always be fair. This desire to be the judge extends beyond childhood games. We are inclined to judge others in real life. Some of us make a habit of trying to read the hearts of others so that we might judge their motives. Truth is, only God knows what really goes on in a person's heart.

There are situations in which God gives a measure of authority to individuals who are called upon to serve as a kind of judge (for example, a governor, a judge, a teacher, or a parent). He nevertheless remains the source and master of that authority. Those who are called upon to make judgments regarding the innocence or guilt of others do so because God has given them a share of his authority. These individuals are expected to carry out their God-given responsibility by focusing their efforts on seeking both justice and mercy.

THREE HUMAN CONFLICT-MANAGEMENT TOOLS

Among sinful human beings, it is sometimes necessary to intervene in a potential conflict by negotiating a settlement. Negotiation is a conflict-management strategy in which two opposing positions work toward a resolution by means of *trade* and *barter*. Each side has to be prepared to makes sacrifices to achieve peace. Parents and teachers often use this technique in an effort to teach children to negotiate their own settlements, without the help of a third party.

Another valuable tool for settling a dispute is through mediation. A *mediator*—a trusted individual whom both parties have agreed upon—keeps the parties working together toward a settlement. Sometimes negotiation and mediation can be combined.

A third human approach to conflict management is called *arbitration*. Arbitration also makes use of a third party—an individual who is empowered (often by law) to determine a final judgment. Arbitration normally results in a clear winner and loser. Parents and teachers have the moral (God-given) authority to arbitrate disputes between children.

While all three of these conflict-resolution strategies are wonderful tools for keeping peace, God's approach to peacemaking involves *repentance, confession, absolution,* and *reconciliation.* Restoring peace in this way *(reconciliation)* is the only approach to conflict resolution that has the power to heal a broken relationship. ▪

DISCUSSIONS FOR CHAPTER SEVEN

1. Describe a recent time in which you discovered that your child was engaged in conflict with a playmate, a sibling, or a parent.

   • What approach did you use to help your child resolve the conflict?

2. How does arrogance (the opposite of humility) interfere with a God-pleasing approach to correcting a naughty child?

3. Consider several situations in which *negotiation, mediation,* or *arbitration* might be used to resolve a dispute or maintain the peace.

   • Would reconciliation have led to an even better outcome in any of the cases that have been discussed?

4. Why is Jesus' teaching about turning the other cheek so difficult to apply to one's own life or to the lives of our children?

5. Read 1 John 1:9 and 2 Corinthians 5:18-21. How do these Bible verses, taken in combination, help us understand the value of trying to resolve any human conflict through reconciliation?

   • Why is it important to teach children to articulate their feelings about sins they've committed or sins that have been committed against them by others through using words like *I'm sorry* and *you're forgiven?*

- As a result of this discussion about reconciliation through repentance and forgiveness, what important lesson do you want your child to learn at home and in school?

✝

Nine-year-olds *hope* their ballgame won't be rained out. Teens *hope* for acceptance. Twenty-somethings *hope* to find a soul mate and be blessed with children. Parents *hope* their children will be successful. Grandparents *hope* to meet all their grandchildren. We all hope for something. And our hoping is intense. Carl Sandburg wrote, "Nothing happens unless first a dream." Emily Dickinson called hope *the thing with feathers that perches in the soul.* Visualizing our future is endemic to the human spirit. We all dream of eternal happiness.

Every parent hopes that his or her child will succeed in school and in life. Our reason tells us that they will turn out just fine if they can learn to make good friends, find acceptance among their peers, stand firm in the face of challenges, and learn to cope in a rapidly changing world. We nod our heads in agreement to the suggestion that our young people *are* the future. We envision them contributing to a world that produces enough food to feed the world's burgeoning population, achieves world peace, or eliminates disease, crime, or poverty. Our hope is brimming with optimism. But it is tempered by disappointment, heartache, and broken dreams. None of these great visions has ever been realized.

The hope of an immortal future is by far the noblest of all human dreams. Because our hope rests in God's sure promises, the Christian educational model satisfies the ardent hope that flutters in our souls.

PART
TWO

"If only for this life we have hope in Christ,
we are to be pitied more than all men."

1 CORINTHIANS 15:19

CHAPTER EIGHT

From Promise to Hope

Most schools declare their reasons for existing in a brief document called a *mission statement*. A school's mission statement identifies the content and approach to learning that its administration and teachers embrace. Good schools accurately reflect what their mission statements assert. The statement ordinarily does not change from year to year. It is a declaration of promise, telling you that this school is committed to the educational philosophy that its mission statement describes. Schools that are committed to the governing principles of *Christian education* proudly highlight their convictions in their mission statements.

THE PARENT-TEACHER PARTNERSHIP
When you enroll your child in a school, you are in reality agreeing to work together with the school's teachers and administration. Some schools even require parents to sign a contract that states the basics of this agreement. Your partnership with the school's teachers and administration commits you to the same educational approach that has already been documented in the school's mission statement. Parents and teachers generally agree to communicate openly and honestly with each other regarding learning objectives, progress reports, school climate, behavioral matters, the curriculum, and other school-related concerns. This home-school partnership is based on trust. It implies mutual respect for each other's God-given roles. It is tempered by patience and love.

The parent-teacher partnership is a dynamic relationship. A healthy and vibrant parent-teacher relationship enhances the child's learning environment and pays rich dividends in terms of learning productivity.

God says, "So that you, your children and their children after them may fear the LORD your God as long as you live by keeping all his decrees and commands that I give you, and so that you may enjoy long life . . . impress them on your children. Talk about them when you sit at home and when you walk along the road, when you lie down and when you get up" (Deuteronomy 6:2,7). The teachings that God is speaking about are written on the pages of Scripture. God wants parents to be active participants in their children's education. This is especially true for the religious education of our children. Christian schools assist parents in their awesome responsibility of training and equipping kids for life. But they can only do so insofar as the children's parents are willing to advance their children's spiritual training at home.

PARTNERSHIP BREAKDOWN

Healthy, vibrant partnerships require time, commitment, and effort. When one or both parties are unwilling to do the work, the relationship is destined to deteriorate. On the other hand, when both parents and teachers are carrying out their God-given roles to the best of their ability, the blessings will be obvious. Here are five indicators that can be used to determine if a partnership is beginning to erode. *Partnerships break down when*

1. *partners no longer perceive each other as equals.*

2. *the terms of agreement erode.*

3. *the agenda is not communicated clearly.*

4. *one or both parties are unable or unwilling to accept responsibility or culpability.*

5. *partners ignore the real issues.*

YOUR CHILD'S TALENTS AND THE COMMUNITY

Among the highest of parental goals is the hope that our children's natural talents, inclinations, and abilities will be noticed. If your child excels in math, for example, you will want your child's teachers to work hard at developing the interests and skills that give your child the best chance for success in math. Why? Because we all want our children to learn in ways that will benefit them in life. But it is also true that we want our kids to someday grow up to make contributions to the communities in which they live. The Christian education model anticipates this parental desire, placing a high value on both the individual and the community.

One of the distinguishing marks of Christian education is its appreciation for a wide diversity of gifts and talents. Christian education advocates the biblical truth that God has gifted each individual with a unique set of talents, abilities, and interests. The Christian education model promotes the idea that these gifts should be developed in ways that can be used to serve other people within the community.

The Bible uses the metaphor of the human body to teach us that every individual has been given a place and a purpose within the community of God's people (the church). In Scripture the body of believers is viewed as a unit that is made up of many parts. One person is an eye; another is a foot; a third person might be an internal organ. All of the parts contribute to the greater welfare of the whole body. Each part must contribute to the body's health and well-being according to its assigned function. If all of us were eyes, there wouldn't be enough of a support system to complement our ability to see—no heart to support blood flow to the eyes, no brain to interpret the images captured by the eyes, no skull to house the ocular system. By itself the ability to see would be quite meaningless.

We need one another. We cannot afford to discredit or demean other parts of the body; we need every cell doing its share of the work.

Children need to understand that God has created each of them as a unique individual. Christian schools teach that every child can contribute to the community's greater good. They emphasize this concept at every opportunity by encouraging students to discover their own personal talents and by showing them how to put their unique skills, talents, abilities, and interests to practical use within their community of friends, families, schools, and churches.

When the sinful self sows the seeds of jealousy, pride, or dissatisfaction among children, they need to be reminded that their personal gifts are unique gifts that God has given for the benefit and blessing of the body of Christ. When children are reluctant to apply themselves to developing their gifts because they are lazy or because they feel their gifts are inadequate, Christian educators will lovingly remind them that their gifts come from God. God is wise in all things and offers such gifts to them in love. They will be reminded that with every gift comes a responsibility to be a good caretaker of that gift. Stewardship of our personal gifts includes growing in ways that will make each gift even more valuable than when it was first received.

The Bible teaches us to identify, develop, and use our personal gifts for the good of the community. One of the most important goals of Christian education is to lead children to the understanding that with every gift comes a God-given purpose. The purposes that God has assigned to the gifts he gives provide a sense of worth and meaning to the young lives of our children. In other words, in the Christian education model, *every child matters*. And every child should know that he or she matters. The communication between parents and teachers is vital in helping children identify their gifts, develop them, and put them to good use.

THE PROMISE OF YOUTH

When God created the universe, he gave the gift of life to humankind in a very special way. He formed Adam from the dust of the earth and breathed life into his lungs. He created Eve from a rib that he had taken from Adam. He placed human beings into an environment in which the passage of time made a lot of sense. For human beings, remembering the past is a valuable asset.

Our memory tells us a lot about who we are today and how we have become who we are. Secular world history chronicles mankind's intellectual progress. Biblical history reveals how God has taken an active interest in mankind's spiritual journey. It shows that our Creator-God has intervened in our human history to insure that his great dream of redeeming us from sin's curse will not fail.

But human beings also have an interest in knowing the future. We plan for the future. In many ways we live for the future. Our decisions are frequently made with the future in mind. Yet none of us has the ability to foreknow our future. We can speculate, but only God knows your future, or mine, with any certainty. Anyone who claims otherwise is either a liar or a fool.

At the beginning of a new season, it is easy to believe that one's favorite team will play in the World Series. The future always looks the brightest at the beginning. As parents observe their child at play, they can envision their child doing great things someday. But many of the dreams we entertain for our children's futures will not pan out as we had hoped. The promises of youthful new beginnings are never a sure bet because we cannot predict the future for our children or ourselves. We may pretend to have some control over their futures, but life just doesn't work that way.

Christian education acknowledges this truth. The Bible tells us that our future (and the future of our children) is in God's hands. In Christian schools, children learn that their future hope rests in a loving God whose promises never fail, even when human promises may often disappoint us. In a world of broken promises, the Christian education model presents the biblical view that we can be absolutely certain of a glorious future in heaven. This blessed future rests entirely on the work that God has done for us in Christ Jesus. We have God's Word on it. Our eternal future is secure. Together with our children, we can be sure that God has forgiven our sins because of the excellent sacrifice that Jesus made on Calvary's cross on our behalf. Because of Christ's own resurrection from the dead, with the eyes of faith we know that we will one day rise from our graves to a certain future in heaven's unending glory.

The word that is often used to describe this certainty is *faith*. Christian education is dedicated to helping your child's faith in Jesus grow. ▪

DISCUSSIONS FOR CHAPTER EIGHT

1. Take a close look at the mission statement of your child's school. Are there elements of this document that you find particularly striking?

   • Have you learned anything that you didn't know before reading this mission statement?

   • Why is it a good idea for parents to know what the mission statement of their child's school states?

2. What kinds of issues can cause a parent-teacher partnership to deteriorate?

   • What can concerned parents do to keep the parent-teacher partnership strong and vibrant?

   • What can a teacher do to accomplish the same ends?

3. React to this parent's statement: *"All I want is for my child to turn out."*

4. Why is it so reassuring to know that God will never lie to us or change his mind about the promises he has made to us in his Word?

5. Read 1 Kings 8:56 and 2 Corinthians 1:20. List as many of God's promises as you can to which he has been faithful.

- As a result of your study of these two texts, what important lesson do you want your child to learn at home and in school?

CHAPTER NINE

A Focus on Excellence

Many schools champion educational excellence. Only the best schools deliver.

Schools that adhere to the model of Christian education have a compelling reason for striving to meet high educational standards. It is worth taking a moment here to examine why Christian schools strive so hard to achieve high standards. To explain this, we will need to revisit the Bible's account of what happened in the Garden of Eden.

When God created the first human beings, there was a strong family resemblance between the Creator and the creature. Adam and Eve were the proverbial *apple of God's eye*—the pinnacle of God's creation. It would be fair to say that everything else that was a part of God's great creative work was made for the blessing and benefit of mankind.

The greatest blessing that God gave to Adam and Eve was the unique way in which he made them. They were holy and righteous in every way, just like their Creator—a chip off the Old Block, at least in spiritual terms. The Bible calls this state of perfection *the image of God.* Made in God's very own image, our first ancestors were in perfect sync with God's holy will. In their pristine garden home, Adam and Eve appreciated their Creator. He continually provided for their physical, emotional, and spiritual needs. They worshiped him with their deepest devotion. Nothing about their high regard for him was artificial or phony. It flowed from a free will that desired only to please God and glorify him in everything they said and did. They were excellent in every way because His Excellency was their Creator. And he was pleased with their excellence.

WHEN EXCELLENCE WAS LOST

Then they sinned. They envied their Creator. They wanted to be in charge of their own lives. Like a row of dominoes, when the first sin had been committed, it was accompanied by a second and a third. In the blink of an eye, God's entire created universe had fallen under sin's curse. For Adam and Eve, the most devastating reality of a world now tainted with sin was the loss of their Creator's image. Suddenly, the first man and the first woman were nothing like their Creator-God. They were flawed. Where their thoughts had exclusively been focused on righteous ideas, they now entertained evil—lies, deception, resentment, jealousy, bitterness. They felt guilt and regret for the first time. They experienced fear. They were self-absorbed. Worse, their excellent, trusting relationship with the Creator had been shattered. In their shattered state, they viewed God as an enemy.

Suddenly they knew that they would taste death. God had warned them that death would be their punishment. He had not created them to die; God is the author of all life; he abhors death. But his perfect sense of justice demanded that they must die. It was his own prescribed penalty for their disobedience.

But God still loved Adam and Eve. Long before he began creating our universe, God already had an excellent plan for dealing with mankind's problem with sin. The plan called for God himself to complete every requirement of his own righteous law. Then, instead of making us pay the penalty for our rebellion, he would personally accept the verdict of guilty for himself, as though he had committed all of those offenses. This plan flowed from God's own gracious love for sinners, who had shown that sin had obliterated their capacity to love him in return.

As despair began to settle in for Adam and Eve, God quickly shared his plan with them. It offered such a powerful kind of hope that it overcame their despair. God promised to send his dear Son into their sinful world. His Son would arrive with divine authority and truth. He would overcome the death grip that sin, death, and Satan had on us. The Son would be God, coming from God—excellence heaped upon excellence!

The biblical account of God's covenant with sinful mankind is all about God's excellence. This narrative doesn't directly explain why we strive for excellence in our schools, but it does explain our drive for seeking excellence in general. By seeking excellence, we are *thanking God for the excellent gift of salvation that he has given us in his Son, Jesus.*

The Bible is very clear in telling us that nothing we could ever say or do could ever repay God for what he has done for us. Besides, you and I don't really have anything that God wants. But we can show our appreciation by being obedient to his commandments, by sacrificing our old habits and sinful tendencies, by leaving our lives of sin. For those who trust in God's promises, this obedience is no longer a demand; God's law is no longer the motivating force of *do this or else.* This obedience is instead a response to God's goodness—a thank offering coming from a heart that has become one with God's will. God says, *"Give me your most excellent offerings. I will help you. But do it because you want to, not because you have to. Do it because you love me in the same way that I have loved you, not because you are afraid of what I will do to you if you don't keep my law."*

While we are driven to excellence by the gospel, none of us will ever achieve perfection in this life. Nevertheless, God's supreme act of love changed everything. He raised to life souls that were dead. He awakened within us the image that had been lost. In heaven that *image* will be fully restored and we will be completely excellent again—remade in God's own perfect image, just as he created us. With his help we can strive each day to be more like his excellent Son. In heaven he will say of us, "You are my son, my daughter, I am well pleased with your excellence because I am well pleased with the excellence that my own Son has achieved for you."

It doesn't matter if a believer is a farmer, an electrician, an engineer, a student, or a classroom educator; giving God our best effort—striving for excellence— is a way of giving glory to God's name. It is glory that is well deserved—glory that rises far beyond the standards we human beings have set for excellence in our imperfect world.

RIGHT MOTIVES . . . AND WRONG

The contrast between a Christian's motivation to achieve excellence and the motivation that the unbelieving world uses to achieve greatness is stark, but not always obvious. One Bible narrative tells the story of a historical event that illustrates the sharp distinction between secular motivation and gospel motivation. The event happened long ago in the ancient city of *Babel*. The event was recorded by an inspired Hebrew historian named Moses—the same Moses of the ten plagues, the exodus from Egypt, and God's giving of the Ten Commandments. You can read his account of the Tower of Babel in Genesis chapter 11.

In the centuries that followed the great flood, Noah's descendents moved south from the mountainous terrain where the ark had come to rest. A vast, well-watered plain (present-day Iraq), where the soil was rich and the climate was favorable, became home for a growing population. The land was ideal for advancing new technologies, especially for cultivating grain crops. Many had forgotten God's gracious act of saving Noah's family. Their appreciation for God's current blessings also waned as their ability to invent better ways of doing things increased. Several other new technologies were being introduced at the same time. People learned how to make kiln-fired pottery, and eventually they perfected the technology for firing clay bricks that could withstand any kind of weather. They also discovered that they could communicate over great distances and with less confusion when they scratched recognizable marks on clay tablets. They invented a new recipe for mixing tar, asphalt, and pitch to create a new kind of mortar that was stronger than any other brick-bonding materials. These innovations were blessings from God. But most of these people didn't see it that way. They believed their superior ingenuity was the reason for their cultural progress. Now they could construct taller, larger, stronger buildings that would soar above the rest of their city. Soon the best engineers and architects in Babel were laying plans to build a tower that would dwarf all of the towers in neighboring cities. And they weren't shy about declaring that the motivation for their ambitious project was to "make a name" for themselves and their city. Babel would soon be famous.

God knew these people were driven by the self-gratifying glory of fame and acclaim. They had forgotten how the Lord God had saved mankind from utter annihilation by placing Noah and his family safely into the ark. God would not stand by idly and let runaway human pride take all the credit for things they could only accomplish with his help and using his resources. He knew that if their disobedience went unchecked, they would forget about him entirely and their hearts would become hardened in wickedness. So God put an end to their wicked plans for greatness by confusing their ability to communicate with one another.

Mankind still has a difficult time learning the lesson that God was teaching to the people living in ancient Babel.

RELATIVELY EXCELLENT

Human excellence is a relative proposition. It is impossible for imperfect people to produce anything that is absolutely perfect. The educational corollary is that there is no such thing as a perfect school. It simply does not exist. Nor will it. The people who populate schools are all infused with sinful desires. The good news is that God loves us in spite of our sinful desires. The fact that he came to earth to live and die to restore the relationship that was broken by sin in the Garden of Eden gives us a profound reason to develop schools that testify to our appreciation for all that he has done for us. When schools are striving for educational excellence, so are its students and their parents. But good schools do not let this effort for achieving excellence happen merely by chance. With their administration taking the lead, controlling boards and dedicated faculties spend untold time and energy planning new ways to achieve a high level of excellence. ■

DISCUSSIONS FOR CHAPTER NINE

1. Make a list of things that mankind lost when Adam and Eve fell into sin.

2. What lesson was God teaching to mankind when he put an end to the building of a great tower in Babel?

3. Create two more lists, one to describe some reasons for striving for excellence that are not biblical. Then create a second list that describes reasons for striving for excellence that are biblical.

4. How can parents and teachers train children to give glory to God for all of their achievements without taking the joy of personal accomplishment away from them?

5. Read Colossians 1:3-12 and Matthew 5:16. In what specific ways can we glorify God's name for all that he has done for us?

   • As a result of your study of these passages in Scripture, what important lesson do you want your child to learn at home and at school?

CHAPTER TEN

Measuring Student Development

Each child grows at his or her own personal pace. The principle that governs this individual growth rate in children applies to *physical, intellectual, social,* and *emotional* learning. This may also be true of the way in which we grow spiritually, but faith is a difficult thing to measure. (Only God knows *how* or *when* or at *what rate* faith matures.) We'll focus first on measuring intellectual (academic) growth in areas of the curriculum such as math, science, history, the arts, literature, grammar, composition, geography, and foreign language studies. Later in the chapter we will consider ways to view the spiritual development of our children.

MEASURING LEARNING BY MAKING COMPARISONS

Diversity is a beautiful feature of God's creation. Life would be very boring without it. But when it comes to learning, diversity creates problems that are often magnified in a school environment.

The *business* of education is far more cost effective when learning is approached as a group process.[1] For this reason, schools are notorious for looking at children less in terms of the individual and more in terms of groups. In a group setting, such as a classroom, teachers have historically applied the same learning standards to all of the members of the group. Individual time-tables, private interests, or personal aptitudes have been largely ignored. In practical terms, learning has been a one-size-fits-all proposition. In such a learning environment, someone is bound to be left behind because he or she is not ready to master skills or subject content as quickly as the other members of the group. On the other hand, a few students may run ahead of the pack, eager to advance at their own speeds.

---

[1] In general, only the wealthy can afford to place their children into educational settings that feature a one-to-one teacher-to-student ratio. In this learning dynamic, the learning curve is slavishly subject to the pace that one student is capable of sustaining. When the dynamic includes more students per teacher, the teacher is forced to make choices that will inevitably compromise someone's learning pace.

Thankfully, during the last few decades, education has been moving in the direction of individualized learning. Economic realities still dictate that most children will have to be taught in school groups, but today's educators are far more aware of the needs of each individual student.

A natural byproduct of the group approach to learning is the tendency to compare students. Such comparisons can be especially helpful in identifying kids who will need special attention and consideration. Diagnostic tools can be used to help educators develop specific *independent educational programs* (IEP) for such students. IEPs help teachers make necessary strategic adjustments in order to meet a child's specific learning needs.

Christian education views children as Jesus views children. He sees every child as a unique, one-of-a-kind individual. Each of their unique characteristics came from the talents, attitudes, abilities, virtues, and interests that he personally gave to them when they were born. Other talents and abilities were still to be developed. The gifts he gives to one child are different from the gifts that other children have received. And, as if that were not enough, Jesus has also lovingly established the timetable for each child's learning curve. His timetable will govern the pace for everything a child masters in a lifetime of learning.

GRADING SYSTEMS AND PERIODIC PROGRESS REPORTS

Throughout the last century, one system of measuring student progress *(A, B, C, D,* and *F)* found wide acceptance. Letter grades are universally understood as a baseline for meaningful conversations regarding student progress. These conversations between teachers and parents are vital for developing sound learning strategies for each child. Additionally, many colleges and universities look at grades and grade-point averages to decide if a student is eligible for admittance.

As popular as the *A–B–C* system has been, it has its share of flaws.

One glaring defect is that it is not always clear if a letter grade represents a teacher's subjective opinion or serves as a composite of scores from daily assignments, tests, activities, etc. Teachers have a responsibility to describe their grading standard to parents so that they are speaking the same language whenever they are communicating about a child's academic progress.

Classroom grades raise awareness. They monitor learning. They inform the dialog. They cause us to ask intelligent questions. But grades also have the potential for being misunderstood and used incorrectly. While a grade can indicate that a student is not doing well in a particular subject area, it does not explain *why* the student's grade level has fallen. Sometimes parents and teachers make assumptions or come to conclusions that are based on suspicion (the child is lazy; the child has a poor attitude; the child has a learning deficiency; etc.) and not on fact. Such assumptions have the potential to undermine a student's morale. Actually, there are a lot of possible reasons to explain why a student's grades have fallen.

LEVERAGING GRADES TO MOTIVATE STUDENTS

Some people use grades to motivate. The idea is to alternately use a combination of sticks and carrots to embarrass or reward a student to achieve at a higher level. Leveraging grades in this way may be done with the very best intentions. But in the extreme it is a recipe for potential abuse. Using grades to motivate a child to do better in school can lead children to despair. It can breed animosity, hostility, and resistance toward authority and learning.

A much healthier understanding of academic grades sees reported grades as a source of encouragement for students. It encourages students to reach for excellence out of gratitude for the blessings of God's love. Seeking academic success is a wonderful way for a child to say *thank you* to God and give glory to his name by applying time, energy, and a godly work ethic to using God-given talents. When children are motivated by the power of the gospel, they find joy and purpose in learning.

MEASURING APTITUDE AND MANAGING A STUDENT'S CURRICULAR PATH

During the last century, volumes have been added to our understanding of how children learn. Within large student populations, we can identify benchmarks in learning. Tools that can accurately measure potential learning strengths are used to determine where a student's *aptitudes* (learning strengths) lie. Such information can be used to set a curricular path that will give each student the best possible chance for experiencing success.

In the Christian education model, measuring academic potential can provide very helpful information. Since Christian educators see each child as a unique individual, much attention is given to finding the best track that will promote success through the curriculum choices that are made for each student. Such information is balanced with an understanding that God alone knows how he wants to put any child's talents to good use.

GRADE LEVELS

When a child's formal education begins (often in kindergarten), most of the children in the same class are about five years old. Many states require that a child must turn five years old on or before a specific date to make the child eligible for enrolling in a kindergarten program. (The dates vary from state to state, and they may even vary from one locale to another.) By policy, some schools allow parents to decide between enrolling an eligible five-year-old in the same year in which they turn five or waiting another year before enrolling. The decision rests more on the child's social and emotional maturity than physical or intellectual maturity.

EARLY ADVANCEMENT AND RETENTION

Occasionally grade placement becomes an issue because a student's ability does not seem to fit the age group to which he or she was originally assigned. The practice of *skipping* or *repeating* a grade is an important decision that deserves thoughtful and prayerful consideration. The child's parents and teacher(s) should work together toward achieving consensus. The only legitimate criteria for considering a move in either direction is whether it will benefit the student.

CHILDREN WITH LEARNING DISABILITIES

Much progress has been made in placing children with special learning needs into classrooms with their (same-age) peers. Addressing the social and emotional needs of kids with learning disabilities is as important as focusing on their intellectual and academic development. Like all kids, children who find learning a challenge need to have a sense of belonging. They need to know that they are an important part of this microcosm of society, which every classroom is. Teachers often adjust assignments, learning outcomes, grading systems, and teaching strategies to accommodate the learning needs of children with special needs.

CASE STUDIES

Teachers are in a good position to observe a student's behaviors. An alert educator may decide to seek the advice or opinions of other professional educators regarding concerns for a child who is exhibiting unusual behavior. Parents have a right to expect that such conversations will be conducted in a confidential, professional manner and always with the child's best interests at heart.

In certain situations (such as in the case of suspected child abuse), state law may require teachers to communicate their concerns to responsible civil authorities. Concerns for a child's behavior may also lead to more formal discussions called *case studies* or *casework*. These studies can involve members of the teaching staff and/or school administrators. Case studies may also be conducted when a student is exhibiting a pattern of troubling behaviors or when there is a serious concern about a situation in the student's private life that may be hindering the child's ability to learn.

A casework team can also include specialists from other fields, such as pastors, physicians, family counselors, social workers, and child development specialists. Casework notes and documents that relate directly to each specific case are kept on file. Parents have a right to access the information contained in their child's file.

In general, parents are not usually included as members of a casework team. But their input should certainly be sought, and they should be kept abreast of any findings, conclusions, or strategic decisions that their child's casework team is considering.

REFERRAL

Some case studies may lead a casework team to conclude that the child's parents should seek the help of a field specialist (family counselor, child psychologist, psychiatrist, etc.). The approach a field expert may take in helping a child with behavioral or personal issues is often influenced by the expert's own personal religious convictions. Parents are encouraged to be bold in seeking information about a specialist's religious affiliation. A specialist whose personal beliefs align closely with the parents' religious beliefs is philosophically better equipped for helping a child overcome challenging patterns of behavior.

MEASURING FAITH

Christian schools offer a style of education that pays a lot of attention to the spiritual needs of children. In a Christian school, your child will learn Bible stories and passages from Scripture that apply to daily life. Some Christian schools require children to memorize texts from the Bible or hymn stanzas that reflect the truths of Scripture. Many Christian schools also include catechetical instruction as part of their junior high or middle school curriculum. In fact, virtually everything that is taught in a Christian school will be richly seasoned with the truths found only in God's Word, the Bible.

Some of the things learned under the heading of "religious training" are cognitive in nature—biblical terms, biblical names, places, events, story details, etc. This kind of learning can be measured, and some Christian schools do attach a grade to this kind of work.

At another level, however, Christian education does not exist to teach Bible facts. In the end, Christian education is all about bringing children to Jesus, building their faith in their Savior, and leading them to grow in their understanding of all that God has done for them. Let's consider an example.

Charles, a child with Down syndrome, was thankful to be attending a Christian school that recognized that he could learn in spite of the challenges that every child with that condition faces. As the other fourth graders in his class recited memory passages or responded to tough questions about the truths of a Bible passage, Charles sat quietly paging through a picture book that told the story of Jesus' life. When he arrived at a page that depicted Christ's crucifixion, his eyes welled with tears. He motioned his teacher to come closer so that he could tell her something quite personal. Pointing at the picture of Jesus on the cross, he whispered, "For me?"

Charles understood the lesson. His faith was growing, yet his progress could never be adequately communicated with a grade. ■

DISCUSSIONS FOR CHAPTER TEN

1. Share an experience with grades or report cards from your childhood.

2. Perhaps at one time or another you have thought that your child was ahead or behind in certain areas of development. What can parents do about such observations?

3. What factors shape a child's attitudes about learning?

• How can a parent help reshape a child's negative attitudes about learning and school?

• How can a teacher help reshape a child's negative attitudes about learning and school?

4. Is it appropriate for a parent to compare a child's progress in school with his or her own school experiences? Explain.

5. Read Matthew 19:13-15. What wonderful insight into Jesus' attitude regarding children does this text give us?

- Read Matthew 18:5,6. Child abuse can take many forms. God's commandments and Jesus' own words clearly show that any kind of abuse is sin. In what way is the subject of this passage a serious kind of child abuse?

- Read Psalm 34:11. According to this psalm of David, what kind of education should Christian parents hold in the highest esteem?

- As a result of this study, what important lesson do you want your child to learn at home and at school?

CHAPTER ELEVEN

Teacher Excellence

Having high expectations for our children's education requires a lot of confidence in the men and women who teach our kids. Their skills, abilities, attitudes, and dedication are the real difference makers when it comes to the quality of your child's education. In this chapter we will consider the qualifications and philosophies of instructors who serve in schools that follow the Christian education model.

To begin, it must be said that there are many Christian men and women teaching in public and private schools who serve as living models of faith to their students. Many of them actively seek private opportunities to share their faith in Jesus with the children they serve. However, state law prohibits teachers in the public sector from promoting their Christian faith as part of the school curriculum. They cannot teach a course of Bible stories or talk openly in a classroom about what the Bible teaches. State law also prohibits them from using a combination of biblical law and gospel to discipline children or motivate them.

A UNIQUE TEACHING PHILOSOPHY

The difference between a school that views life and learning from a law-gospel perspective and a school that can only see life and learning through the lens of the law is an important distinction. Secular classrooms are limited to carrying out discipline or motivating their students without the benefit of the good news that Jesus died to forgive sinners. They can teach the differences between right and wrong, but moral living is not the ultimate goal of the Christian faith, nor is it the central message of God's Word. Christian schools can, and do, make full use of both the law and the good news of forgiveness in Jesus to correct, comfort, and encourage students. This factor definitively sets Christian schools apart from schools that follow a secular model. In fact, this factor separates Christian education from all other educational models. Under the Christian education model, a teacher approaches discipline with both the law and the good news of God's forgiveness. A child who feels the burden of guilt and is sorry for wrongdoing needs to hear that God still loves him or her. For that student, the law *and gospel* approach makes all the difference in the world. Similarly, a teacher in a Christian school can encourage students to work hard and learn according to the gifts they have been given. But not because it is demanded of them (a manifestation of the law). Rather, they will work hard and learn out of gratitude for the many gifts that God has showered on them, especially the gift of salvation in Christ Jesus.

TEACHERS MOTIVATED BY THE GOSPEL

If it is true that the good news of salvation in Christ is at the heart of a Christian school's disciplinary and motivational approach, it is also true that the same gospel drives the work ethic of educators who teach in a Christian school. They are there because they too are sinners who know they have been reconciled with God through the redemptive work of Christ Jesus. Christian educators are motivated by the gospel, even as they use that same gospel to motivate their students.

With God's good news of eternal life as their chief motivation, Christian educators have an abiding concern for their students. They frequently find themselves wrestling with God, asking him to help them discern those situations when it is appropriate to apply a word of admonition or correction (law) to children who may be apathetic about their sin or to speak a reassuring reminder of God's love (gospel) to children who are hurting from a guilty conscience and need to hear about God's forgiveness.

Christian educators pray for their students, knowing that God has promised to give them *anything* they ask for in Jesus' name. They strive to be fair in all things and with all students. They are eager to show mercy and kindness. They radiate a joy for life and an appreciation for the opportunities they have to serve others. They let their light shine so that parents and students can readily see Jesus living in them. Their earnest desire is to lead children to Jesus and his love.

Some children seem to go out of their way to make it hard for their teachers to love them. Christian educators make a special effort to love these kids. They are patient and willing to listen. They know that having strong and loving relationships with kids that are hard to work with will give them opportunities to connect these children with their Savior.

Christian educators love children, all children. Their professional goal is to spend eternity in heaven with all of the children that they have had the privilege of teaching.

At the same time, it must also be said that Christian educators are not perfect people. They sin. Yet they are humble. Christian teachers know that God forgives them for Jesus' sake. They regularly study God's Word to be refreshed by the never-ending fountain of God's love. They are faithful in attending worship services and eager to join with other Christians to focus their attention on Jesus and his saving work. They know their Savior in a personal way. He is their spiritual nurturer. They cling to him in the same way that a branch remains attached to its life-sustaining vine.

PREPARING STUDENTS FOR THIS LIFE

While Christian teachers are always concerned for the spiritual well-being of their students, they are also deeply concerned about their professional goal of preparing their students for this life. They grow in their skills, learning new teaching methods and techniques so that they can become even more effective in the classroom. They are interested in increasing their knowledge and have a high regard for learning. They further their formal education so that they can do a better job of giving children the tools they will need to survive in a competitive environment.

Professional Christian educators mentor one another, sharing educational insights, encouraging one another, praying for one another, supporting one another, and, if necessary, correcting one another. They make it their business to know how children learn. They take their relationships with parents very seriously and work hard at becoming strong partners with the moms and dads of the children they teach. They hone their communication skills and gather strength through prayer for those hard conversations that have the potential for producing conflict.

Christian educators are peacemakers in every sense of the word. They are masters at recognizing teachable moments and taking full advantage of the opportunities such moments present.

Christian educators understand that today's families are often hurried and are exceedingly busy. They respect the time families have for being together. They understand their role as an educator is to support parents in their God-given nurturing responsibility. They honor parents and children, taking the time to listen with a discerning ear, without making judgments that only God has the right to make. They lead with positive attitudes, genuine compassion, and the voice of gospel encouragement. ■

DISCUSSIONS FOR CHAPTER ELEVEN

1. Tell the other members of the group about one of your favorite teachers from your childhood.

2. *(For parents)* Describe the ideal teacher. What things could you learn from professional Christian educators?

   • *(For teachers)* Describe the perfect parent. What could you learn from the parents of the children you teach?

3. How can parents encourage the teachers of their children to continue to grow in faith, in knowledge, and in love?

   • How can Christian educators encourage parents to keep growing in faith, in knowledge, and in love?

4. Read 1 Peter 5:2-9. From this text make a list of attributes that every Christian educator should have.

   • Which of these characteristics would you place at the top of your list? Explain why.

CHAPTER TWELVE

Measuring Your Child's School

Today's schools bring people together from a broad spectrum of ethnic, socioeconomic, and geographic backgrounds. The Christian education model blends this melting-pot stew into a school culture that is distinctively *Christian*—a culture that ideally glows effervescently with the brilliant light of the gospel. The Bible does not provide specific learning theories, teaching methodologies, or suggestions for curriculum. Yet everything that happens in a Christian school connects with the Christian faith. All learning theories, methodologies, and curriculum that are part of day-to-day life in a Christian classroom serve the greater spiritual truths of Scripture. Yet they are as practical as they are spiritual.

Since the foundation for the entire Christian education model is the Bible, the overarching standard for measuring organic life in a Christian school ought also to be God's Word.

CURRICULUM

Kids learn a lot of things in school. Some of their learning is very intentional. Some learning happens with little or no planning. *Curriculum* is the content package of all the planned learning that is supposed to occur in a school. A school's curriculum might even *intentionalize* some of the unplanned things that will be learned. A general curriculum in today's American culture includes mathematical disciplines, such as arithmetic, algebra, geometry, and calculus. Language studies—such as reading, spelling, and composition—are also common offerings. So are studies about the earth and its people—geography, social studies, anthropology, history, foreign languages, classical cultures, philosophy, the fine arts, music, the plastic arts, theater, literature, woodworking, mechanical engineering, physical education, health, consumer education, etc.

A curriculum is structured around a menu of specific learning objectives and outcomes. School administrators and faculty advisory groups often work in tandem with parents to construct a curriculum that suits student needs.

Curriculum study committees influence the selection of textbooks and supplemental resources. They also determine the number of hours allotted to each subject.

In a rapidly changing world, schools tend to adjust their curriculums often. (How many high schools still offer a typing course?) It is important that content remains current and is supported by technologies that are kept up to date.

In recent decades technology has played an ever-increasing role in determining teaching techniques and methodologies. Interactive white board technology is a contemporary example of a classroom innovation that is currently sweeping the nation.

A *balanced* curriculum is considered favorable, though how the word *balanced* is defined always makes for an interesting (and sometimes contentious) conversation among educators. In general terms, attention to balance in a school curriculum gives children a chance to grow in a variety of disciplines and interests.

Standardized tests can help schools maintain their curricular balance by identifying areas of a program that need attention. Such tools can also highlight areas that are worth building on. Teams of professional educators can also help a school identify strengths and weaknesses in its program. The process of seeking certification, accreditation, or licensure often requires on-site team visits.

A school administration can also conduct internal self-studies to examine a school's performance in specific areas. These studies may range beyond the purview of curriculum to evaluate other aspects of school life, such as building cleanliness, staff professionalism, the nutritional value of foods served in the cafeteria, code compliance, or protocols for safety alerts, fire drills, and other emergency procedures.

A CURRICULUM ROOTED IN HISTORY

The book you hold in your hand reflects the religious convictions of the Wisconsin Evangelical Lutheran Synod (WELS for short).[1] As the name indicates, WELS represents a branch of Lutheranism.

The founder of the Lutheran church was Martin Luther. Luther was, among other things, an outspoken proponent of Christian education and a champion

---

[1] Currently there are approximately 775 schools throughout the United States and Canada that are owned and operated by WELS congregations. This includes preschool programs, elementary schools, middle schools, high schools, and colleges.

of children and learning. Luther believed that Christian education begins in the home and that the primary responsibility for the spiritual nurture of children is implicit in the role God gives to parents. Luther also understood that the historical elements of Scripture explain how God's saving plan unfolded over time. The Reformer believed that the Bible's accounts of the patriarchs, Israel's judges and kings, Jesus' life on earth, and the beginnings of the New Testament church demonstrate God's faithfulness in all things.

The curriculum in WELS schools provides many opportunities for children to learn these precious Bible narratives.[2] The study of Bible history is an important part of the curriculum in a Christian school—one that clearly sets Christian education apart from the secular model.

The Lutheran (Christian) view of history stands in stark contrast to the secular view. Secular historians focus on man's accomplishments and the human obsession with managing the future by studying the past. This approach to understanding history is based on the notion that history repeats itself in patterns and that our knowledge of historical patterns can help us determine future outcomes. Where history is taught from a secular perspective, human hope is rooted in the false belief that man can control his own destiny.

The Christian faith, on the other hand, is rooted in the reality that God is the Creator of time and change and that all of human history is under his divine authority and control. Lutheran Christians believe that, with one exception, it is impossible to know with any certainty what the future holds. The singular exception is that those who trust in God's promises know with complete confidence that their future has already been secured for them in heaven. This truth is clearly taught in God's Word. It is a tenet that Christian education fondly embraces and fervently proclaims. In a Christian school, your child will hear this biblical assertion repeated many times over.

CULTURAL VIEWS THAT CHALLENGE BIBLE TRUTHS

Every aspect of a Christian school's curriculum reflects Bible truth. All subjects are taught from the understanding that God is active in every facet of life on our planet. He governs. He guides. He causes change. He gives life and sustains it. The theory that describes the origin of the universe as an evolutionary process, for example, does not line up with what Scripture teaches. It must be

---

[2]The historical narratives that are found in the Bible are sometimes referred to as *Bible stories*, though they are not fictional literature as the word *story* often implies.

challenged on the premise that God's Word always communicates absolute truth and mankind should never dare to add, subtract, or alter anything in it. In WELS schools the biblical record of creation is taught literally. Your child will learn that the universe was created by God in six 24-hour days.

In Christian schools, Bible truth is taught exactly as God intended it to be taught. Difficult topical subjects—such as human sexuality, gender identity, abortion, and divorce—will be discussed honestly, openly, and in an age-appropriate way. More important, all of these conversations will take place in the light of what God has to say about these topics in his Word. Where our culture addresses moral or ethical matters in ways that are contrary to Bible truth, the partnership between parents and teachers is critical in helping students grasp the issues from a biblical perspective. Preparing the next generation of God's people for life in a hostile cultural environment means that parents and their teacher partners will be wrestling with the very same topics that their young students are wrestling with.

SCHOOL CLIMATE AND CULTURE

Like snowflakes, no two schools are exactly alike. Each has its own unique thumbprint. Each has a distinctive climate wafting through its halls, through its classrooms, and on the playground. In good schools this climate is manifested in the positive attitudes students display as they go about their daily business of learning. In good schools positive attitudes reside in the students' healthy relationships with one another and their teachers. In good schools students and their instructors are confident in their abilities to solve problems, overcome obstacles, and address challenges. Positive attitudes are a natural byproduct of a healthy school climate. But it could also be said that a healthy school climate is the natural byproduct of positive attitudes.

A healthy school climate often holds a handful of core values in high regard. One school's core values may revolve around a strong work ethic. In another school the core values may emphasize compassion for people in need. In still another school there is a high value placed on social interaction and cooperative learning. In another there is an emphasis on leadership. Some schools work especially hard at being open and transparent. Others take pride in their child-centered approach or have a reputation for encouraging a lot of parental involvement and participation. Where schools make the effort to stand out by fostering positive attitudes, the results are generally observable and favorable.

In Old Testament times, nothing unclean was permitted in the tabernacle (or later in the temple), where God *resided*. Every knife used to prepare the sacrifices; every ceremonial utensil used to sprinkle the blood on an altar; even the tables and show bread, the lampstands, and fragrant incense—everything had to be set aside and purified, never to be used again for ordinary household applications. Even the priests were consecrated (set apart) to serve God and his people as they carried out their priestly duties. These ordinances were pictures of how God's people were to see themselves. They were to be unique, different—people set apart from the rest of the world—God's people.

To the casual observer, a Christian school may look like a carbon copy of a secular school. For a keen eye, the climate of a Christian school stands out in stark contrast with other schools, because the people who populate a Christian school know that Jesus is there with them. They know their Savior is watching over them and protecting them from temptation. They seek nourishment and encouragement from his Word. They bask in the warmth of his love, knowing that he has cleansed them with his forgiveness and will strengthen them in a time of difficulty. The climate in a Christian school is uniquely different because Christ and his Word touch everything. Jesus is the difference maker. ▪

DISCUSSIONS FOR CHAPTER TWELVE

1. Make a list of observable characteristics that make your child's Christian school stand out as distinctively different.

2. Can parents have an impact on a school's curriculum decisions?

   • Do parents in your child's school have enough opportunities to have input in curriculum development?

   • How can parents become more involved in the curriculum development process without impinging on the role of Christian educators?

3. What core values seem to rise to the top in the culture of your child's school?

• What core values would you like to see receiving more attention?

4. Do you agree or disagree with this statement? *In Christian schools, Jesus is the difference maker.* Explain your answer.

5. Read 2 Corinthians 10:3-5. Why is it so important for Christians to stand firm on the Scriptures and not allow false ideas to seep into the things we teach to our children?

   • How can we "take captive every thought to make it obedient to Christ"?

   • Read Jeremiah 29:11. What absolutely sure view of our future does God himself promise in this text?

   • As a result of this Bible study, what important lesson do you want your child to learn at home and at school?

CHAPTER THIRTEEN

Hope for This Life

The educational model found in Christian schools is a complete package. It not only prepares students for finding a good job or starting a successful career, it prepares young people to withstand the "hurricanes" of life.

You and I can shelter our kids from life's harsh realities for only so long. Sooner or later illness, disease, warfare, poverty, grief, or any one of a hundred other challenges is sure to make an unwelcomed visit. Satan works tirelessly to crush the human spirit. He knows that adversity can cause people to abandon hope. His purpose is to drive us and our children away from God. One of his favorite strategies is to put us into the path of one of life's most devastating hurricanes.

A DESERT TERRAIN

While Satan's strategy is to steal our hope, God has an unusual strategy for helping people who are trapped in hopelessness. He takes them to a wilderness place. There, in a fiercely hostile environment, he teaches us to have hope in his promises. Hope has its basis in miracles and in God's ability to make good on his promises to overcome what otherwise would be impossible odds. In the wilderness, miracles matter.

The people of Israel had lived in Egypt for about four hundred years when an arrogant Pharaoh rose to power and forced the Hebrews to labor under cruel taskmasters. After sending ten plagues (each a miracle in its own right), God delivered his people from their slavery. Then he took them into the desert where there was no food or water and little reason for hoping to survive. Why would God do that to the people he loved? In the vast nothingness of the desert, they would learn a vital lesson—their survival and well-being weren't dependent upon the forces of nature or their own cleverness. Their survival depended on God alone. It would be the height of folly to turn their backs on God.

On a mountaintop in the middle of the Sinai wilderness, God gave his Ten Commandments to Moses. These commandments outlined what God expected from the Israelites, whom he had just delivered safely on dry ground through the waters of the Red Sea, drowning Pharaoh's army in the same waters. The commandments that God prepared for his people were a gift. God wanted them to live in a way that would please him and give glory to his name. But while Moses was on the mountaintop receiving the Ten Commandments from God's hand, at the base of the mountain, God's chosen people were worshiping a golden calf—an idol. Their response to the God of their deliverance was to spit in his face. And later they spit in his face again when they refused to take possession of the land God was giving them. So the desert became their classroom. In the desert they had nothing to give him to earn his favor. Yet, in one spectacular miracle after another, God showed them that there was hope for those who believed his promises. There, in the wilderness, they could see God providing an endless supply of everything they needed for their daily sustenance. Daily he offered his right arm of protection from their enemies. Daily he gave them food and water to sustain them. Daily he provided his forgiveness for their time-and-time-again failures to trust his promises. Day in and day out God was faithful, even when his people were not. At the end of their 40-year trek, he led them into a land flowing with milk and honey, just as he had promised.

THE BROKEN DREAM

There are times when God's people need to remain in a bleak desert environment for a while, but not as punishment for disobeying his law. Hard times in the desert have the salutary effect of forcing us to do some serious soul-searching. One awful truth in particular needs to be confronted. The truth is that none of us is the person God wants him to be. Neither can our children ever hope to meet God's perfect standards. God's law drives that reality home. His law convicts us. Against the standard of God's commandments, we fall short of the mark that he has set. Our sinful hearts take us in the opposite direction, on a trajectory of recklessly pursuing hell. Sin forfeits our great dream—the dream of a joy-filled, eternal future with God in heaven. The tragic fact of sin is enough to leave us all wallowing in hopelessness and despair.

Painful as it is, acknowledging our sin is the first step in reconnecting with our God of hope. In a hostile desert environment, the people of Israel learned to recognize their lack of trust and to rely on God to meet their physical, emotional, and spiritual needs. In our personal wilderness places, we too learn to recognize what we are and in whom we can trust.

FROM HOPELESSNESS TO HOPEFULNESS

Our desert wastelands come in many shapes and sizes: the loss of a dear friend, a bout with depression, a heart attack, test results that confirm a cancer diagnosis, a broken marriage, a failed business, an unwanted pregnancy, a job loss, the news that a son or daughter in the military will be serving in a dangerous place, a bitter divorce. A child's troubles often seem less threatening and sometimes even quite petty: a bully on the playground, disappointment at not getting a part in the school play, an injury that sidelines the young athlete, the death of a family pet. But for children, these are real desert experiences.

Our personal trials have a way of taking us into a bleak desert landscape of loneliness, grief, guilt, shame, indecision, or fear. At the same time, they have the potential to drive us back to the safety of a loving heavenly Father, where we can find healing and hope. He wants our children to know where to go for the hope they need when life's circumstances become unbearable. "Come to me all you who are weary and burdened," invites Jesus, "and I will give you rest" (Matthew 11:28).

Christian education prepares children for the challenges of life. The Christian education model acknowledges that God frequently sends people into our lives to intervene. He blesses us with extraordinary resources to help us when the pressures of life seem unbearable. And he promises to be with us and to strengthen our faith when hope is hanging in the balance. God's promises are the bedrock of Christian education, because his promises offer real and lasting hope.

When children sense that they are threatened, their first instinct is to run and hide. That is just what our first parents did when the shame of their disobedience brought them to the brink of despair. Adam and Eve sought cover, fearful that their Creator would destroy them.

God found them. And, in perfect justice, he pronounced his perfect and just judgment for their disobedience. But he did not take away their hope. Instead, in the dark new realities of life on a sinful planet, God gave them a reason to be hopeful by promising to send a Savior who would miraculously undo their disobedience.

Spiritually speaking, we are still running away from God. Since the fall, the human race has consistently turned away from God's promise to help. Blinded by our sinful condition, mankind has been inventing alternative strategies to God's offer. Sadly, the human solution is to abandon *hoping* in favor of *coping*.

I GET BY WITH A LITTLE HELP FROM MY FRIENDS

For some people hopelessness is just too painful to think about, so they work hard at being satisfied with dumbed-down, plain-vanilla dreams. They have convinced themselves that, for them, dreaming big of an eternity in God's loving embrace isn't productive.

Others look for a way to prop themselves up when hope has all but vanished. This solution offers the illusion that *all is well.* Sadly, when the hangover wears off and the party has moved to a new location, the hopelessness remains.

With wealth comes a certain degree of freedom. It helps us cope in a world driven by material things. But wealth only lasts a little longer than the drug of choice. Many a dishonest stockbroker has helped a lot of investors realize that one's portfolio isn't a good place to look for lasting hope.

Power creates the illusion that one can manipulate events. But even the most powerful kings on earth are subject to God's will. Anyone looking for real hope will have to come to grips with the fact that the almighty God has a will that supersedes theirs. He will have his way, and no power on earth is able to resist it.

There are those who travel through life hoping against hope that they will be more fortunate than others. Lady Luck is fickle. Learning that the chances of surviving bypass surgery are better than 90 percent can be a reason for hope— unless you're among the 10 percent of the bypass population that does not survive. The only sure bet is having odds that favor you one hundred times out of one hundred chances. Odds like that are called *miracles.*

SEEING HOPE IN GOD'S MIRACLES

Peter had spent the better part of three years with Jesus. He followed his teacher everywhere. He saw blind people receive their sight, folks dying from leprosy made healthy and whole, crippled individuals walk again, demons cast out, and deaf mutes suddenly hear and speak. On three separate occasions, Peter saw Jesus raise lifeless cadavers to life. Twice he saw his master produce enough food to feed thousands of hungry people.

One day a man who specialized in collecting the temple tax asked Peter if his rabbi was planning to pay his annual temple tax.

Peter had seen Jesus pay the tax in previous years. "He is," replied Peter.

To avoid causing offense, when they were alone, Jesus told Peter to go to the Sea of Galilee, throw out a line, take the first fish he caught, and open it's mouth. There, in the fish's mouth, Peter would find a coin. "Take the coin to the tax collectors to pay our tax," said Jesus.

Talk about odds! Jesus knew the precise location where Peter needed to drop a hook. He knew that the first fish caught would have a coin in its mouth and that the coin's value would equal the exact amount needed to pay their temple tax.

By definition, a miracle is an event contrary to the laws of nature and regarded as an act of God. Where human experience is concerned, miracles don't happen. Where the Almighty is concerned, they do. Jesus did many miracles. He did them as proof to support his claim that he is the Son of God. But there was another reason why Jesus did miracles. He did them to keep people's hope alive.

Hope is always open to the possibility of miracles. Hopeful people expect impossible things to happen. They have a positive outlook about everything in life. They see God's blessings surrounding them. They see a future that stretches far beyond the pain and suffering of this life.

The most hopeful people on earth are those who know that God will make their greatest dream—immortality with their Lord Jesus in heaven—a reality.

The Bible says, "With God *all things* are possible" (Matthew 19:26). That is a remarkable claim—one that stretches the limits of human hope. Christian education is rooted in this kind of hope. Such profound hope transcends the limits of human accomplishments. ▮

DISCUSSIONS FOR CHAPTER THIRTEEN

1. Have you ever seen a real miracle? Explain.

2. Do you see evidence in your child's young life to support the assertion that Satan is trying to crush the human spirit and cause even a child to despair?

3. Many of the Bible stories that your child will learn in a Christian school make reference to miracles. Why are miracles so important to a Christian's faith and hope in God's promises?

- How can parents and Christian educators help children develop a healthy, godly view of miracles?

4. Describe a time in your life in which you think God may have taken you into a desert wasteland. What truth do you think he was trying to teach you?

- How did he bless you as a result of the experience?

5. Read Genesis 32:22-32. How do we find real and lasting hope when we wrestle with God?

- Do you agree or disagree with this statement? *One of the great privileges of being a Christian parent is teaching a son or daughter to seek blessings from God by wrestling with him often.* Explain your answer.

- As a result of this study, what important lesson do you want your child to learn at home and at school?

CHAPTER FOURTEEN

Hope in the Resurrection

Hopelessness is by far the most devastating problem confronting the human race. It is so disheartening that we go out of our way to shelter our children from the blunt realities of life for as long as we can. We don't want them to give up their naive hope just yet.

The underlying issue for our hopelessness is death. If this assertion seems overstated, consider how unsettling it is for us to deal with death. Consider how far out of our way we will go to protect kids from having to face this reality at an early age. This chapter connects the dots between Christian education and the sure hope for a complete victory over death.

The Bible's sole purpose is to restore hope to sinners like our children and us. When God's Spirit breathed life into that lump of clay, the living man he brought to life was perfect, just like his Creator. Endowed with a free will, just like his heavenly Father, Adam brought glory and praise to his Creator's name. But that perfect relationship didn't last. Sin turned Adam and Eve's righteous attitudes upside down. Suddenly they resented God's fatherly providence and rejected his loving embrace. Worse, they had no way of their own to overcome the terrible curse that had come as a result of their own willful disobedience.

Neither do we. You and I get a sense of our own hopeless condition when we take the time to evaluate the dark thoughts, loveless conversations, or disgusting behaviors that also appear in our lives. Sin permeates the human soul.

A holy and just God cannot simply ignore the wickedness that has taken over our lives. But he has addressed it. In fact, he has fully resolved the impasse that separates us from his loving embrace. God's answer to the human condition of hopelessness was both just and loving. He gave us the gift of hope by giving us himself.

Hope has a name. It is *Jesus*. Some of the very first lessons your child is likely to hear at a Christian school will be about Jesus. Children learn how Jesus arrived on our planet through a miracle (conceived in the womb of a virgin), how his arrival was announced in a miracle (proclaimed by angels and declared in the movement of a remarkable star), and how he miraculously returned to his permanent home in heaven (ascended into the clouds). The whole concept of God coming to a sinful world to live as a man, in time and space, is a mind-boggling miracle that is impossible for the human brain to grasp fully. When it comes to dreaming really big, the only name to turn to is the name *Jesus Christ,* God's Son. We can, with our children, dream the dream of immortality in God's perfect heaven because God dreamed the divine dream of saving the entire fallen human race.

THE GREATEST MIRACLE

The greatest miracle our world has ever seen is the miracle of love. But without God, our world could never grasp either the concept of love or the miracle it produced.

Love is much more than a tired romantic expression; it is an act, a behavior—a way to conduct one's life. Love has purpose and intent. It is a dynamic force that drives, motivates, and produces radical change, always for the good. Love gives, and it keeps on giving.

The Bible tells us that "God *is* love" (1 John 4:16). Love has its origin in God. Love and God are inseparable; one cannot exist without the other. God's love for us is personal. He extends his love to you and me in very intimate ways. As an expression of his deep love for us, God sent his only Son (whose human name is *Jesus*) to live on earth among sinners. Jesus came into a world that scorned him, denied him, despised him, and murdered him. In a very personal way, he accepted your death sentence, giving you his righteousness and holiness in exchange. God sacrificed the life of his only Son on a cross *for you.* In that sacrifice God put his love into action for you. Because of his sacrifice, you can one day stand before your eternal judge, unashamed and without a hint of sin to stain your image.

In this exchange your heart (the dead and hardened heart of a sinner) was transformed into a heart that is vibrant and alive with God's love. God's love is the reason you have hope. His love is at work in your heart and in your life right now.

You and I have not earned the right to be treated in such a loving way. We deserve, instead, to be squashed like a mosquito on God's neck. The hope you and I cling to for a meaningful and satisfying future is a gift of the highest value; it is wrapped in God's personal love for us.

You and I cannot fully grasp God's great love. Such love cannot be measured or contained. We can, however, see it in action. God's love is not a mystical presence; it is tangible and observable. In Christ Jesus, God's love took on the form of human flesh and blood—a miracle, yet also tangible and observable.

The Bible's true account of Jesus' suffering and death is the key to understanding God's love. Hearing about the final days of Jesus' life, we begin to grasp the depth of God's love. But from that Good Friday narrative alone we would still have great difficulty finding a reason to have hope. The problem is *death*.

THE REALITY OF DEATH

Death is a reality you and I face every day. We see it all around us. We see the creeping signs of it in our aging bodies. We all know how final death is. Because of death, it's hard for mortal human beings to put our hope in anything that reaches beyond the grave.

On that dark Friday when Jesus hung suspended between earth and heaven, his followers saw their Savior as a broken man about to draw his final breath. Everything they had dared to hope for was lost. All of Jesus' promises suddenly seemed empty. What tangible reason for hope is left when the Savior they had bet the farm on is rotting in a grave? Where does one go then to find new hope? The apostle Paul said that if we only have hope in Christ for this life, we are to be pitied more than all men (1 Corinthians 15:19). How true! After three years of being together with Jesus, hearing him teach, watching him do one incredible miracle after another, his followers still could not see a reason to have hope for the time *after* their dead bodies would be laid to rest. What a pity! They were no different than the rest of us. Death's finality makes us throw our hands up in despair, asking, *Is that all there is?* Death is the real reason for our hopelessness.

Three days after his crucifixion, the dead Savior, whose lifeless body had been sealed in a tomb, raised himself to life. Jesus had told his followers this would happen. They just had a hard time believing him. It seemed too good to be true. Only a fool would entertain the outrageous notion that we might somehow prevail in our lifelong battle with death. Yet, if it could be true and immortality were within reach, wouldn't that change everything? Wouldn't you awake every morning relieved by the unexpected surprise of having real hope for a future overflowing with perfect peace and endless joy?

The Bible's Easter story of Christ's resurrection is true. Jesus is alive. He conquered death—*for you* and for the other members of your family. Even if your time of grace ends today, the future is still yours. His resurrection assures us that we too will rise. This powerful victory over the grave is again a gift of God's love. Free! No strings attached. It is a miracle that only God could pull off.

God planned for you to have the miracle gift of everlasting life even before he created the world. He wants your children to have it as well. With Christian education as your partner, your child will hear the accounts of Jesus' death and resurrection over and over at home and at school. Christian schools and Christian parents are united by the good news message that Jesus is the living water that refreshes and renews hopeless souls. Through the simple washing away of sin in the waters of Baptism, God assures parents and children alike, *"You are my dearly loved child."* In love, God provides the hope for you and the other members of your family.

Is there hope? Absolutely. We have every reason to be hopeful because the hope that we cling to—the hope that comes from God's promises—is a sure hope. Our hope in Jesus' resurrection is foundational to the philosophy of Christian education. In Christ Jesus we have an eternal future in heaven. There we will be reunited with all the saints. There we will be with our Savior-God forever. It is hope based on the reality of the empty cross and the vacant tomb. This hope will sustain you and your children for the rest of your journey through this earthly desert. Better still, it will transport you across the threshold of the grave to the heavenly place where your eternal future is waiting. ▪

DISCUSSIONS FOR CHAPTER FOURTEEN

1. Has your child had any encounters with death? If so, how did your child react?

2. What hopes and dreams do Christians cling to when unbelievers settle for a far lesser dream?

3. When death touches the lives of students attending a Christian school, what kind of comfort might you expect from their teachers? from their fellow students? from God's Word?

4. Discuss the significance of the fact that what happened on Easter is a historical event.

- Discuss Easter as a truth that we can apply to our own lives and the lives of our children.

- Discuss Easter as a reason to celebrate at home, at school, and at church with fellow believers in the resurrection.

5. Read 1 Corinthians chapter 15 (all of it). This is one of the most important chapters in the whole Bible. It is filled with many bits and pieces of information about the resurrection that give us hope. After reading it, what important lessons (you may name more than one) do you want your child to learn at home and at school?

✝

During his two bids for the presidency in 1984 and again in 1988, Jesse Jackson held his political rallies in poverty-stricken neighborhoods. Before his formal speeches, the candidate would invite inner-city teens to come forward, most of them beaten down so badly by the oppressive squalor and peril of the inner city that they lacked any positive attitudes about themselves. For a half hour the candidate would lead them, rhythmically chanting the same three words until many had lost their voices: "*I* am somebody! I *AM* somebody! I am *SOMEBODY!*" As the minutes wore on, the impact was palpable. Heads lifted. Shoulders squared. Eyes brightened. The din grew in intensity until the pavement shook. Jackson understood how young people long for a sense of self-worth. He instinctively knew how much they want to matter.

Understanding who we are and how we fit in is critical to healthy human development. For most people the struggle to find themselves begins during childhood. It can be an intoxicating ride or a miserable debacle.

When asked, many parents will say, "I just want my child to be happy." They are not trying to be vague or evasive. These parents instinctively know it is important for their child to be accepted by teachers and have friends; to find satisfaction in learning new skills, exploring new ideas, and having new experiences; to have a sense of control over their lives; and to influence the lives of others—to, in fact, be *somebody.*

We all want our kids to find joy in the lives they have been given. As our conversation about Christian education continues, we will turn our attention to student self-awareness and self-expression. Under the general heading of *JOY,* we will consider the approach that Christian education takes toward the development of a healthy *personal identity.*

PART
THREE

"Come, let us sing for joy to the Lᴏʀᴅ;
let us shout aloud to the Rock of our salvation.
Let us come before him with thanksgiving
and extol him with music and song."

Psᴀʟᴍ 95:1,2

CHAPTER FIFTEEN

The Joy of Being

The Bible teaches that all life has its origin in God's infinite creative power. Christian education upholds the principle that life is a precious gift and deserves our utmost respect.

The Fifth Commandment is very specific regarding the way God wants us to value human life. In a Christian school, your child will learn to make this commandment an important part of his or her personal worldview. In this chapter we will look at the joy that God wants us to have when we know why he has given us the gift of life.

Just about everyone eventually asks, *Why am I here? What am I supposed to do with the life that God has given me?* Our children often wonder what God's purpose is for them. For young people, whose personal identity is still in its developmental stages, the question *What do I want to be when I grow up?* is healthy.

The Bible teaches that "we are God's workmanship, created in Christ Jesus to do good works, which God prepared in advance for us to do" (Ephesians 2:10). The apostle Paul, the inspired author of this letter, was talking about children as much as he was talking about adults when he penned these words. Christian schools and homes work together in tandem to help children understand that . . .

1. *God has a master plan for all of his people;*
2. *God has assigned a meaningful role to me in his plan;*
3. *God is preparing me for carrying out the purpose he designed just for me;*
4. *God places me into the perfect position to carry out my role;*
5. *God promises to be with me and bless the work that I do in my role;*
6. *God is not obligated to share the details of his plan with me or to show me the results of my work. His expectation is that I trust him to lead me in carrying out his will.*

Did you notice that all six of the lessons began with *God?* While he gives us our lives and provides lots of choices along the way, *who we are* and *what we do* with the time that he has given us rest entirely in his hands. That view is very different from the way the secular world approaches life. It is one very important reason to say confidently that the Christian education model is distinctively Christian.

IDENTITY: *DOING* AND *BEING*

Strike up a conversation with a total stranger, and it won't be long before someone asks, *What do you do?* Identifying people in this way may seem superficial, but the formula works surprisingly well in social situations. Most of the time we are temporarily willing to forego any deeper understanding of one another. We'll settle for an easy handle to remember the person, knowing that perhaps later we'll explore the things we may have in common.

We all understand how this dynamic affects our children. A child who excels in sports, music, or spelling catches the attention of others. We encourage our children to *do* well, though we silently hope they will also *be* well. We proudly display primitive works of art on the refrigerator door and collect countless ribbons and certificates to celebrate the little successes. A lot of work goes into shaping their public personas. Our emphasis is generally on the things our children *do.*

There is a downside to placing so much attention on the things our kids *do.* When children see how important it is to their parents that they *do well,* they may begin to forget who they *are.* And this could lead to a major identity crisis. Many young people are keenly aware of what they can (or cannot) do, but many haven't a clue as to who they are.

Identity is a composite of *being* and *doing.* Knowing who they *are* is prerequisite to helping children develop skills and abilities that will allow them to do things well. They are, after all, human *beings,* not human *doings.*

Family is the right place to help a child establish a healthy understanding of *who I am.* Kids need to know that they belong to a family that surrounds them with love, provides for their needs, and gives them support. They also need to understand their personal identity in terms of gender: *I am a boy* or *I am a girl.* They need to know what it means to be male or female before they have to deal with questions about how boys and girls act and interact in social settings. Similarly, kids need to have a cultural point of reference: *I am an African-American* or *I am of Hispanic ancestry.* When children identify with their own national, racial, and ethnic origins, they begin to see how they fit into the bigger picture of humanity. When children see themselves in this way, history and tradition suddenly become much more meaningful. They can begin to see *how* and *why* they belong.

Christian boys and girls have a personal identity that is based in their baptisms. Our kids are who they are because of God's undeserved love for them. In their baptisms, they became members of God's eternal family. They belong to God, citizens of his eternal nation of believers. Their identity is informed by their faith in Christ Jesus. They bear his likeness, the image of God lost in Eden and restored to them in Jesus' life, death, and resurrection.

SELF-WORTH

We all need to *be somebody*. We crave self-worth.

Saint Paul wrote about what he knew of himself. He said, "What a wretched man I am!" (Romans 7:24). Paul said this because he saw himself as *the problem*, not just the sorry wreck that was the result of a problem. As *the problem*, Paul knew he could not be part of *the solution*. The apostle was reminding us that, in and of ourselves, we have no worth. At least, we have no worth in God's eyes—in the minds of other human beings we may seem to be wonderful people.

Paul was right. On our own we are not capable of producing anything of value or worth to God. And no one in the world can change that. Making us worthy to be in God's presence is the kind of job that only God himself could take on. And he did, sending his own dear Son into our sinful world to *do* what we could not.

Our self-worth is wrapped up in Jesus. We (and our children) need to value ourselves as God values us. If being a sinner makes me worthless and unable to do anything that will please God, then what I need is a new identity. Paul wrote, "I have been crucified with Christ and I no longer live, but Christ lives in me" (Galatians 2:20). What that means is that you and I are somebodies because of Jesus! I am a child of God. So are you. In Christ we have a significance that is complete and perfect. The apostle also wrote, "For to me, to live is Christ" (Philippians 1:21).

Self-worth has little to do with pats on the back, money in the pocket, friends in a network, points on a scoreboard, or grades on a report card. Our children need to know that they are worthwhile because Jesus is worthy in the eyes of his heavenly Father. On two separate occasions, Jesus' Father said so publicly: "This is my Son, . . . with him I am well pleased" (Matthew 3:17; Matthew 7:15). And in the final pages of Scripture, we read, "Worthy is the Lamb" (Revelation 5:12). Those words are speaking about *the Lamb of God,* Jesus. Because of his sacrifice, every child of his can sing:

> *I am Jesus' little lamb;*
> *Ever glad at heart I am,*
> *For my shepherd gently guides me,*
> *Knows my needs and well provides me,*
> *Loves me ev'ry day the same,*
> *Even calls me by my name.*

VICARIOUS JOY

As an elementary school principal, I especially enjoyed visiting the lower-grade classrooms. Few pictures are more breathtaking than those of children learning to read and write. On this particular day, the assignment was to write *a letter.* Jason caught my attention. "I'm writing a letter to my mother," he stated with conviction. I saw the unbridled joy in his face as he etched a vertical line that looked like a section of old road on a map. Then he plowed a second furrow perpendicular to and near the bottom of the first line—making a crude capital *L* perhaps.

Seconds later a pear-shaped *O* took shape about two furlongs away from the *L,* followed by a leaning *V* and a much smaller inverted *E,* which floated several inches above the other letters. Jason's grin was big enough to melt the Grinch's heart. But I was the one experiencing joy.

A second word of five more imperfect uppercase letters required several more minutes of the same ferocious energy that had been applied to the first four letters. When the youngster was finished, we were both exhausted. His *letter* consisted of two words: *LOVE* and *JASON*—nine total letters. No additional number of letters could have communicated a more profound message. This was a work of art, an expression of pure joy! ▩

DISCUSSIONS FOR CHAPTER FIFTEEN

1. A Bible text quoted in this chapter says, "We are God's workmanship, created in Christ Jesus to do good works, which God prepared in advance for us to do." Explain what a good work is and how it is possible for sinners like us to do good works that please God.

- In reference to this text, explain what you now know about the purpose God has prepared for your child.

2. Make one list that notes things your child does to make you a proud parent.

- Make a second list that includes reasons why you are thankful for the kind of person your child is becoming.

- Which list dominates?

- Are you comfortable with the balance between the two lists?

- What changes would you like to make to get the two lists to balance?

3. Read Galatians 3:26-29 and 4:1-7. What great comfort can we take from these words?

- As God's heirs, what legacy do we have a right to expect?

- After studying this text from Galatians, what spiritual legacy do you want to pass along to your own dear child?

Sing a New Song

Watch your child at play, and you will know what an extraordinary blessing imagination is. From this gift springs mankind's capacity to build skyscrapers, construct bridges and dams, and invent new technologies for space travel, medicine, communication, and transportation. It takes the genius of imagination to write a letter, fly an airplane, invent a lightbulb, discover a continent, defeat smallpox, design robots, or develop a personal computer. Without imagination we would never be able to experience the joy of reading a Shakespearean couplet, hearing a Bach fugue, admiring a painting by Michelangelo, or being immersed in the complex harmonies and rhythms of a Brubeck jam session.

Christian education encourages innovation. It fosters the human desire in our children to follow in the footsteps of the divine Creator; we *create* because our God created us to create.[1] The Christian education model provides an environment that consciously promotes creative thinking. But so does the secular model. Christian education knows that children enjoy invention and self-expression. But so does secular education. So, when it comes to invention and innovative thinking, what sets Christian education apart from its secular counterpart?

Unlike the secular model, the philosophy behind Christian education's passion for developing its students' creative instincts reaches far beyond the earthbound rationale that secular models espouse. Guided by hearts that have been miraculously transformed, our wills align with God's will. Our alignment with God's will is not a perfect alignment. (That will be the case only when we get

---

[1] There is, however, a major difference between the way human beings create and the way God creates. When man creates, his creative effort always begins with materials that God has provided. Music, for example, starts with the building blocks of vibrating sound waves and the physics that make sound possible. It also relies on the marvelous structures of the human ear to be able to capture the vibrations in a meaningful way and a brain that is able to organize the sounds that stimulate its own pleasure centers. When God creates, he literally begins with absolutely nothing.

to heaven.) But as we are transformed, our sanctified imagination is able to generate wonderful new ideas about how to serve God and his people. Christian schools help students discover their God-given talents in a way that will also lead them to consider innovative new opportunities for sharing Jesus with a world that is still living in unbelief.

INNOVATION AND CHANGE

We live in an era of unprecedented change. This is not the normal kind of change that occurs whenever the torch is passed from one generation to the next. The scope of changes that we have witnessed in our own lifetimes comes along only once every few centuries.[2]

Many of the changes in our era, though not all of them, have been the products of new technologies. These technologies were driven by an explosion of new ideas. They affect everything we do—our work, our play, even our approach to learning.

The changes of recent decades have taken most of us by surprise. Some of them are so dramatic that they alter the ways in which we think and interact. Our children and grandchildren will no doubt continue to experience the same accelerated pace of ongoing change during their lives. Preparing children for the rapid pace of change is a challenge for any educational system. Nevertheless, this preparation is not an option anyone can afford to dismiss or ignore.

Knowing that change is a reality of contemporary life, the Christian education model embraces it as a high priority. The model acknowledges that the new signs of rampant change will, in many ways, test our moral resolve. But it also follows the biblical path that Jesus laid before us when he promised to always be with us.

The Christian home and the Christian school serve as living laboratories for children to learn about change and how it affects lives. Change is occurring all the time in both environments. Learning and growth are very important kinds of change. Christian teachers remind their students that God is in control of all things and will cause every life-changing event to serve the good of those

---

[2]The last period in history that saw change as dramatic as the change that has occurred in our era took place about five hundred years ago with the advent of the printing press, Copernicus' unheard-of notion that the sun was the center of the universe, and the profound religious ideology of Luther's Reformation. It was also during this era that Columbus discovered the new world, ushering in an age of unparalleled exploration and the major population shifts that followed.

who trust in his promises. Christian parents encourage their children not to be afraid or worry about the changes that the future might bring. We remind our kids that God is in charge of everything that happens, including those changes in life that blindside us. (See Romans 8.)

At the same time, some human ideas are dangerous and threaten the faith of those who are spiritually weak and vulnerable. God reminds his people to carefully examine every new idea to discern whether it is God-pleasing or not. (See 2 Timothy 4:1-5.)

SALT AND LIGHT

Childhood is a fragile period in the human life cycle. While change is constantly occurring within every child's mind and body, kids themselves are powerless to control anything. As infants they had to rely on adults to feed them, clothe them, provide shelter and security. Even as they grow to be two, three, four, or five, they still have very little influence over their circumstances. Though they may often try, no youngster lives with the conviction that he or she can change the world, or even the tiny little corner of the world in which he or she lives. And yet, the Lord Jesus had the audacity to describe every man, woman, *and child* in his kingdom of believers as an agent of change. Listen to what Jesus had to say about a Christian's relationship with change:

> You are the salt of the earth. But if the salt loses its saltiness, how can it be made salty again? It is no longer good for anything, except to be thrown out and trampled by men.
>
> You are the light of the world. A city on a hill cannot be hidden. Neither do people light a lamp and put it under a bowl. Instead they put it on its stand, and it gives light to everyone in the house. In the same way, let your light shine before men, that they may see your good deeds and praise your Father in heaven. (Matthew 5:13-16)

Jesus is not talking about surviving change or fearing its effects. To the contrary, he sees every person in his kingdom *as salt* and *light.* Both actually cause change.

At one time salt was a very important trade commodity. It changed the flavor of food to make it palatable and kept meat from spoiling. In cold climates, salt thaws ice. Salt changes things. But if salt were to somehow become diluted, it would lose its capacity as a flavor enhancer, a preservative, and a treatment for an icy pathway. When salt loses it saltiness, it is worthless. It would be thrown away.

Our children need to see themselves as the salt of the earth. As salt, they can influence the views that unbelievers have of the dying Savior. As salt, their young lives can have an impact on the behaviors and decisions that others make—even unbelievers.

Jesus also said that the purpose for our lives and the lives of our children is to shine the hope of his promises into the dark places of unbelief. Light draws people to its safety. When a torch is lit on the top of a hill for all to see, it provides a safe haven. The mood immediately changes from fearful to relieved.

The Savior has called on you and me, and our children, to be salt and light—to serve as his agents of change.

The apostle John lived to the ripe, old age of about a hundred years. The people who were living at the time of John's death had not been there to see Jesus' miracles or hear him preach. They had not witnessed Jesus' crucifixion, his victory over the grave, or his ascent into heaven. John had. He was an eyewitness to all of these extraordinary events. John wanted to report what he had seen and heard to the younger generation. He wanted them to know that the name of Jesus meant eternal life for them as well as for the people of his own generation. So John wrote, "We proclaim to you what we have seen and heard, so that you also may have fellowship with us," adding, "We write this to make our joy complete" (1 John 1:3,4).

The world of John's final days was in constant turmoil. Change was everywhere, much like the world in which we live. John wanted that new generation, steeped in change, to know that his personal Savior was also their Savior. And sharing that saving news with the younger generation brought the unexpected blessing of complete joy, even as John waited for God to take him to his eternal home.

Dear parent, you and I can have the same heart-pounding joy that John was describing when we vigorously pursue our children's spiritual training at home and in school.

MY LITTLE GOSPEL LIGHT

When Jesus ascended into heaven, he left his followers behind to do the work of spreading the good news of God's forgiveness to all the nations of the world. Today he is still touching people with that same wonderful news. But he uses ordinary people like us to get the job done. He wants unbelievers, stuck in the hopelessness of sin, to see his compassion living in us. He wants our children to hear from us about the miracle of God's love working in our lives. And he wants our children to pass that same saving message on to the generations that follow. That is our purpose—our life's mission. It is also their life's purpose and mission.

Christian education highlights the joy of taking up this challenge. It encourages young believers to go, preach, and teach. A few will take up that challenge as their life's occupation. Others will use their creative gifts to reach people with the gospel in the arena of their private lives.

Christian schools prepare our children for works of service that bring glory and honor to God's name. He pours out the gift of joy on all who participate in his great harvest. His little ones have a sanctified new song to sing:

This little gospel light of mine, I'm gonna let it shine.
This little gospel light of mine, I'm gonna let it shine.
This little gospel light of mine, I'm gonna let it shine.
Let it shine all the time. Let it shine! ▪

DISCUSSION FOR CHAPTER SIXTEEN

1. What evidence do you see in your child's playtime activity that tells you that imagination and creative endeavor are important parts of what it means to be human?

2. What impact has the fast pace of life or the dramatic changes in our culture had on your family?

   • Do you view either the pace of life or the dramatic change we all have to face daily as positive development, negative development, or merely a fact of life in our era?

3. What major changes have occurred in our world between the time when you were in school and now?

- Does the idea that God's people are all agents of change as salt and light alter your thinking? Explain.

4. Read Genesis 1:26. According to this passage, what was at least one purpose that God assigned to human beings?

- How should these words influence the way in which a Christian school goes about structuring its curriculum?

- Read Matthew 28:18,19. The words of the preceding verse were a general proclamation meant for all people. These words of Jesus were meant only for believers. What great purpose does he give to all of his believers with these words?

- How do these words challenge Christian parents and their children?

- In what ways should these words shape the curriculum of a school that follows the Christian education model?

5. Make a list of things your family enjoys. Is it an exaggeration to say that everything on the list would be second-rate when compared with the joy of telling another person about Jesus?

- After wrestling with these passages from Scripture, what important lesson do you want your child to learn at home and at school?

CHAPTER SEVENTEEN

Celebration Time, C'mon . . .

A dear pastor friend of ours periodically reminds his congregation, "Life is rough; get a helmet." It's a lighthearted way of saying that our journey in life is going to be a mix of good times and bad, celebrations and disappointments. In chapter 13 we discussed the importance of remembering God's promises when we are forced to deal with the hard things in life. In this chapter we will consider Christian education's rationale for teaching children to celebrate both the good times and the bad. This chapter will reinforce the idea that we sing a joyful song for many reasons, even if we have to wear a helmet while doing it.

BEING REAL ABOUT LIFE

Christians are *realists*. God's people understand that the lives we have planned for ourselves will not always be lived out according to our plans. The journey our children are just beginning will be very similar to our own. There will be bumpy patches along the way. The reality is that God's plans are actually better for us than our own. Even when his plans may cause us to hurt, we know that he will bless us and make even the worst hardship or heartache work for our good.

The responsibility to prepare our kids for hard times is a heavy one. How well have you prepared your son or daughter for the day when the news from the lab isn't good, when a natural disaster destroys your home, when a distant war takes a loved one, when a thoughtless act extinguishes the life of someone dear, when unrelenting poverty stifles a child's hope for a decent education, when mental illness paralyzes the entire family, when a broken marriage leads to broken people, when a promising career is ended by a debilitating accident? Our stories may differ widely, but in one respect they are carbon copies. We all face crises in our lifetimes. Our children face the same prospects.

A BURNING QUESTION

During a crisis there is a tendency to wonder *what did I do to deserve this?* It can be a very troubling question. Like their adult counterparts, kids ask the same questions: *Why me? What did I do?*

When faced with a crisis, we immediately begin to search for an answer. How we answer that question makes all the difference in how we deal with the crisis.

While most crises are thrust upon us without much warning, how we view them will determine whether they are going to crush us or not. One person calls the wind damage from a tornado a terrible personal tragedy while his neighbor calls the same sad destruction to his own home an *act of God.*

The Bible discusses in several places why bad things happen. It is worth noting that in every case God's love is always a key to understanding why these events happen.

In the Old Testament, an entire book is dedicated to a study of this question. It is called the book of Job (or just Job). Job is described as a righteous man. As the story unfolds, God permits Job's faith to be tested with a series of personal tragedies. In short order, he loses his flocks and herds, his house, his children, and his own health. Job has good reason to wonder, "Why me?"

Three of Job's friends attempt to provide an answer. But none of them is able to see God's great love working in and through Job's troubled life. They can only see Job's sad lot as the result of God's vengeful punishment for some terrible sin. They advise Job to "curse God and die."

In the end only Job is able to discern the truth. With a remarkable depth of spiritual understanding, he makes a compelling confession. God must have some good reason for all the terrible tragedies that have befallen him. Yes, they were sad. Yes, they caused unrelenting pain and unimaginable suffering. Yes, he was disheartened by it all. But his faith was still intact. His confidence in God's promises was never in danger. As long as Job knew that his loving God was in control, he would never have to suffer the punishment his sins deserved. That singular good and gracious promise from God overshadowed every evil that had ever befallen Job.

The same question came up during Jesus' ministry.

One day Jesus and his disciples came upon a beggar who had been blind from birth. Christ's disciples posed a question they had probably been discussing among themselves. "Rabbi," they asked, "who sinned, this man or his parents, that he was born blind?" (John 9:2). They assumed the man was being punished for some specific sin that either he or his parents had committed. (They sounded very much like Job's misdirected friends.)

But that was not how Jesus wanted anyone to understand this man's blindness. After Jesus had restored the man's sight, he explained that neither the man nor his parents caused his blindness. He could say this because he knew that one day he would take all of the punishment that the blind beggar deserved, along with all the punishment that the blind man's parents deserved, to the cross. The fellow's blindness was never meant to be understood as a punishment. Rather, it was a special blessing. God used this insignificant beggar to make a very important point. Jesus explained, "This happened so that the work of God might be displayed in his life" (verse 3). And it was. Jesus gave the man the gift of sight so that his Father's name would be glorified.

Some Pharisees were sent to investigate this miracle. When they challenged the beggar, he declared that Jesus had to be a prophet. That didn't sit well with the Pharisees. They then questioned the man's parents, who confirmed that the man was their son and that he had been blind since birth. That was not what they were hoping to hear, so the Pharisees hauled the poor fellow in for one more round of questioning. Only this time the frustrated temple leaders insulted the man.

The beggar finally felt compelled to make a marvelous confession. He said, "If this man were not from God, he could do nothing" (verse 33).

CELEBRATING THE HARD TIMES

Any parent or teacher who has had to deal with a child who has just experienced a devastating setback knows these are not happy moments. Even where adult Christians are concerned, it is a rare individual who, in the thick of a painful and disappointing experience, is able to express joy in God's training process. But that is exactly the approach that the Bible takes when it comes to learning how to deal with hard times.

Our children are learning this approach in school when they study God's Word and hear the Bible stories that teach the lesson of godly perseverance. They are taught to see God's love even in the bitterest challenges that life can throw their way. "We also rejoice in our sufferings," wrote Paul (Romans 5:3). Really? Did he say we should *rejoice* in our suffering?

Yes, really. When we are suffering, God's grace is most apparent in our lives. It's the best time to celebrate. Paul also said, "When I am weak, then I am strong" (2 Corinthians 12:10).

CHRISTIANS CELEBRATE

You and I have a lot to celebrate. So do our children. Birthdays recall the blessings of life. Anniversaries remember the blessings of our institutions—marriage or the founding of a new church. We celebrate the birth of our Savior on earth. We rejoice in his victory over the grave on Easter morning. We memorialize his ascent into heaven and the sending of his Spirit to establish his New Testament church on earth. As unlikely as it may seem, we even give thanks for his painful and unjust execution on Calvary's cross.

As citizens who appreciate the blessings of our country's freedoms and the strength of its democratic government, we also take the time to celebrate the birth of our nation, its heroes who sacrifice so much on our behalf, and the work ethic of our citizens. We celebrate the bounty of God's hand in providing for all our physical needs.

Christian education makes a special point of joyfully highlighting all of these celebrated events. It trains young people to celebrate with gratitude and reverence by giving glory to the source of all our blessings.

But the Christian education model also teaches children to celebrate their own personal highs and lows in life—the A that occasionally appears on a report card, but also the accident that happened on the playground; a big win on the athletic field, but also the devastating loss of a friend who transfers to another school. In the final analysis, we are always and only celebrating God's grace. And though we may not always know exactly why he has visited our lives with a troublesome crisis, we can be sure that he has a good reason for doing so. His grace is always there, sufficient to meet all of our needs. It is there, hovering in the background of every joyful song we sing. ■

DISCUSSIONS FOR CHAPTER SEVENTEEN

1. How well did your parents prepare you for the hard things of life?

• What are some of the dangers of being ill-prepared?

2. What are some of the greatest joys of your life?

• How have you celebrated these joys?

3. One family we know sets time aside every day to ask every family member what the greatest blessing of the day was and then to also ask everyone to share a low point in the day. Imagine the benefits that your family could enjoy by using a similar approach to a daily family talk.

- How often does your family celebrate the ordinary blessings of everyday life? (For example, do you pray before or after meals?)

4. Read 2 Corinthians 12:7-10. In this very personal description of a "thorn" from which Saint Paul was suffering, the apostle explains how he can actually find delight in his own weakness. How is Paul's attitude quite different from our own attitudes regarding hardship or disappointments?

- What important lesson do you want your child to learn from this text?

CHAPTER EIGHTEEN

The Gentle Art

One of the great wonders in life is that all of our stories are so similar. We are conceived. Nine months later we pass through our mothers' birth canals and draw our first breaths. We learn. We grow. We mature to adulthood. We work. We engage in creative endeavors. We play. We love. We interact. Some of us marry. Some of us bear children. A few of us make a mark in life big enough to be remembered by the next generation. And then we die. With few exceptions, the path is remarkably predictable. Over and over the stencil of life is reused. And yet, in all this sameness, each of our stories is a profoundly different narrative. Christian education places a high value on sharing all of these wonderful stories with one another. Whether its about sharing our personal stories, making our points, or proclaiming Jesus and his cross to others, the Christian education model sets the bar high for developing students with sound communication principles.

COMMUNICATION LEVELS

Talk is cheap, or so the saying goes. We communicate on several different levels. They are all necessary, but some truly are more valuable than others.

Functional communication is basic. It constitutes the majority of talk around the house and at school. "When are you picking me up from the dentist?" or "Please pass the peas." The wheels of everyday life start to come off rather quickly when we fail to utilize functional communication skills to orchestrate the ordinary happenings of everyday life.

Small-talk communication serves practical social needs. Our common conversations about weather, sports, the latest in fashion, etc., provide us with opportunities to get to know one another better. When we engage in small talk, we can get a reading on how a person is feeling or plant the seeds of a future conversation on a topic of mutual interest. Kids need to learn how to interact socially, using their small-talk skills to open doors to deeper levels of communication.

Beyond the level of small talk, the volume of communication drops off significantly. Deeper, more personal kinds of talk about relationships, personal feelings, or joint problem solving receive far less of our time and attention. Communicating personal issues often takes us into sensitive areas. There's a lot more risk connected to a discussion about hurt feelings than there is in a conversation about the NBA, the NFL, or MLB. We avoid such conversations because we see them as mentally taxing or emotionally painful. Often, in spite of the best intentions, it is these heart-level conversations that fail to happen. Many of us could benefit from special training to help learn the skills and bolster the confidence we need to discuss the really hard topics.

FAITH TALK

One level of communication deserves to stand head and shoulders above all others in the hearts and minds of our children. We'll call it *faith talk.* A Bible writer wrote, "Set your minds on things above, not on earthly things" (Colossians 3:2). This kind of conversation may not always come naturally or easily. We have to learn how faith talk fits into our daily conversations. It takes practice and commitment to foster a pattern of regular God talk. In time it becomes second nature.

Christian schools build opportunities into the curriculum and as part of the school environment for students and teachers to engage in this important kind of conversation.

Spiritual talk can be risky business. It has the capacity to touch a sensitive nerve or to move an individual in a special way. Faith talk is an ongoing conversation about God's loving plan for us. It's talk about sin and guilt and the very real eternal consequences for breaking God's commandments. But faith talk is also about God's love for us in Christ Jesus and our gratitude to him for providing a substitute who would take our sin upon himself and offer his righteousness to us in return.

Faith talk is never cheap. God's children need to learn how important it is to hold his name at the center of their lives.

THE SITTING ROOM

The floor plans for Victorian mansions often included a parlor, a library, and a sitting room. Courting took place in the parlor under watchful eyes. The library was the center for aesthetic and academic development. Music lessons, painting, and letter writing were restricted to this room.

Sitting rooms were usually small. This is where intimate communication took place. Today we build our homes with private rooms, where every member of the family can retreat into solitude. But 150 years ago people were so hungry for conversation that they planned a room where people could go just to talk.[1]

The Christian education model believes that the floor plans for our children's lives need to highlight the importance of communication. God takes an interest in the way his people communicate. We should not be too surprised to hear this; our ability to communicate is another of his extraordinary gifts to the human race. God understands communication. He created us to be social creatures. He gave us the gift of language. He speaks to us in the inspired words of the Bible. And he listens to us when we speak to him in prayer.

The importance of honest, direct, loving communication can never be overstated. The converse is also true. Poor communication can destroy any hope for the things we desire most for our children and ourselves. Sadly, the offices of school counselors are crammed with children and adults who lack the appropriate attitudes and skills to get along with others.

The Bible is filled with inspired advice and encouragement for God's people to communicate effectively. The following list samples some of the more important aspects of God-pleasing communication.

- *Be honest in everything (Ephesians 4:25).*
- *Be loving (1 Peter 1:22).*
- *Honor others above yourself (Romans 12:10).*
- *Be humble; you too are a sinner (Matthew 7:1-5).*
- *Be patient and forgiving (Matthew 18:21-35).*
- *Build others up instead of tearing them down (Romans 15:1,2).*
- *Keep your tongue under the control of a heart ruled by Jesus' love (James 1:26).*
- *Salt your conversation with talk of Jesus and the Christian life (Colossians 4:6).*
- *Talk about things worth treasuring (Philippians 4:8).*

---

[1] To be frank, not all people living in the Victorian era longed for the kind of conversation that sitting rooms were designed to promote. In some Victorian homes, lovely sitting rooms were built without a fireplace. A cold sitting room guaranteed brief conversations.

THE TEACHING PARENT

What joy there is in seeing one generation pass along the truths it has learned to the next generation! Sadly, the age of specialization threatens to rob godly parents of that joy. Somewhere along the way we've sold our parental birthrights for a mess of pottage. We have stood by idly and watched our nurturing and training role erode. (The same can be said for both the secular and the religious communities.) In the process we have forfeited the joy that comes with teaching a youngster to fly a kite, bake cookies, read a map, or build pinewood derby cars. Worse, we have permitted that same flawed thinking to prevail in the spiritual training of our children.

Today *specialists* teach our kids to play games, sing songs, drive cars, avoid drugs, understand sexuality, and construct a value system. The models that dominate today's education landscape (including the Christian model) have siphoned off parental responsibility for nurturing children. In the minds of many people, the home is no longer viewed as a place of learning. We defend our willingness to abdicate our parenting role with flimsy arguments that range from *I'm too busy* to *I'm incapable of teaching my kids much of anything in our complex world.*

Many parents say they feel unprepared and inadequate when it comes to sharing Bible truth with their children. These are godly people. They know that without an ongoing dialog about faith, their household will be missing the one thing no home should ever be without: the good-news story of God's saving love in Christ Jesus. But some parents have never acquired the tools or the confidence to make these vital conversations happen. One parent recently shared that his philosophy is to "let teachers be the experts, . . . parents are responsible for the logistics and making sure their kids get to where they need to go."

Some unhealthy messages are lurking in that kind of thinking. In his Word, God has said that he wants moms and dads to fix his words in their hearts—and teach them to their children. "Talk about them when you sit at home and when you walk along the road, when you lie down and when you get up" (Deuteronomy 6:7). The church and the Christian school have a critical supportive role to play in the spiritual education of children. But Scripture makes it clear—these words are intended for parents.

NO EXCUSES

Our reluctance to teach our children about Jesus at home revisits some old, worn-out excuses:

1. *I'm a poor communicator.*

2. *I'm intimidated by Scripture.*

3. *We are the typical "hurried" home.*

4. *I'm new to the faith.*

There are others. The *age-of-specialization mentality* suggests that mom and dad are not prepared or equipped when it comes to talking about the Bible or sharing their faith life with their children.

Saint Paul never gave the early Christians the chance to hide behind such excuses, even if they were new to the faith. Though he had not yet visited the Christian community in Rome, he spoke strongly of his confidence in them as spokespeople for Christ. "I myself am convinced, my brothers, that you yourselves are full of goodness *[the goodness of Jesus' perfect life]*, complete in knowledge *[the knowledge of their salvation in Christ]* and competent to instruct one another" (Romans 15:14). These are powerful words to encourage parents who long for the privilege of carrying out the spiritual nurturing responsibilities that come with childbearing. ▪

DISCUSSIONS FOR CHAPTER EIGHTEEN

1. Is there a conversation you wish your mother or father would have had with you when you were a child? Explain.

2. From the list on page 102, identify one aspect of communication in your home that could use some work. Look up the Bible text(s), and develop a simple strategy for improving this area of family conversation.

3. Educators often speak about *teachable moments*. These are the golden opportunities for teaching a valuable lesson. How can parents also make use of this profound educational concept?

4. Read Romans 15:14 again. What was the apostle's underlying message in these words?

- Do these words apply to both parents and Christian educators? Explain.

5. Read Proverbs 22:6 and Ephesians 6:4. How do each of these texts sharpen your understanding of your God-given parental duties?

- Based on the message and tone of these two texts, what kind of parent do you want your child to become someday? (What kind of grandparent do you want to be?)

- As a result of your study of these Bible texts, what important lesson do you want your child to learn at home and at school?

CHAPTER NINETEEN

The Joy of Talking With God

When the secular world wants to accomplish something, people place their confidence in human energy and ingenuity. The results can be spectacular: an electric light bulb is invented; man walks on the moon; an atom is split; human DNA is catalogued; the Mona Lisa takes shape as colors converge on a canvas. But putting one's faith in human ability involves some risks. *If* I am industrious, *if* the idea works, *if* my intuition (or my science) is correct, *if* I am able to communicate my dreams to others, *if* I can convince others to follow me, *if* I have the necessary resources, *if* I have a little bit of luck, then maybe my objectives will be achieved.

That's a lot of *ifs*.

When Christians want something accomplished, they place their confidence in the true God of infinite power and endless love. He has promised to hear our prayers, and he has promised to respond to them by giving us what he knows will be best for us. The beauty of it is that there are no *ifs* when God makes a promise. He keeps them all! It's a win-win proposition. So our introduction to Christian education includes the following discussion about the role prayer plays at home and in school in the lives of our children.

AN EXPRESSION OF FAITH

The Bible's simple message of God's grace tells us that he has done what neither we nor our children can do. He has accomplished every spiritual requirement that his perfect justice demands. In love, he promised to send a Savior to redeem mankind from the disgrace of disobeying their own Creator. In love, God kept that promise when he sent his Son into our world. In love, his Son in human flesh lived the righteous life we could not live. In love, his Son took the punishment for our disobedience on himself. In love, God's Spirit claimed us for his kingdom by planting the seed of faith in our hearts. In love, his Spirit also made that faith grow. In love, Christ rose from the dead to give us the hope of our own resurrection to life eternal. In love, he arranged to have the entire history of his plan unfold on the inspired pages of the Bible. In love, he now lives within each of our sanctified hearts. When it comes to our salvation, God has done it all because he loves us. And we are grateful that he has. As sinners we came into this world lacking any spiritual resources whatsoever to accomplish these things, regardless of the amount of energy or ingenuity we would invest.

God knows us well. When he formed Adam from the dust, he hardwired our first forefather with a will that was free to participate in the decision-making process. That freedom has been passed down from generation to generation. As God's people, you and I can make choices, and we can influence the choices that others make. In fact, our free will is so much a part of us that we can't resist the urge to *do* things that could result in lives that are more comfortable or more meaningful.

In his creative genius, God also provided a tool that allows us to literally influence his decisions—to, in effect, exercise our will in his very presence. The tool is prayer. Prayer is the human half of a full-blown conversation with God. It already existed in the Garden of Eden, where Adam and Eve walked and talked with God daily.

Some prayers are requests for blessings we desire for ourselves or others. Some prayers say thank you to God for blessings received. There are times we may feel the need to confess our sins and reaffirm our convictions when we talk with God. And some prayers are very intimate expressions that give glory directly to God. He hears them all. And we bring great joy to him when we come to him with our heartfelt expressions of faith. But these thoughts that we speak *to* our heavenly Father cannot be separated from the Bible, where God *speaks to us.* Without faith in God's Bible promises, even the most eloquently worded prayers are an unbeliever's gibberish. On the other hand, when we are influenced by God's Word, we respond to his promises with the confidence that he will keep his promise to hear us and that he will act on our behalf, as he has also promised. He does all of this *for Jesus' sake.*

DOING THINGS MY WAY

Children typically begin to demonstrate a will of their own around age 2. Someone has dubbed this life stage the Terrible Twos. Any parent will tell you that caring for children of this age requires a double measure of patience. Two-year-olds want what *they* want, not what their parents want them to want. The reality is that all two-year-olds depend on adults for just about everything.

Sometimes we act like two-year-olds in our relationship with God. We want things done *our way*. God may even have to say, "You better let me do that before you make a real mess of things." Thankfully, in our relationship with him, God is *the adult*. He understands our immature behavior. Like any good parent, he gives us a chance to have our say. He invites us to talk to him in the same trusting way that a child might speak to his dear father, even though our will is not yet perfectly in line with his. But here's the important thing: God really listens. In fact, the more you and I engage God in our prayers, the more we will realize that he not only listens but he responds in ways that, without fail, turn out to be blessings.

Getting to that point where we can begin to see how God works for us through the gift of prayer takes practice. We first need to learn to look carefully at what happens when we take our requests to our heavenly Father. Learning to be patient in waiting to see how God will answer our prayers is just as important as the prayer itself.

A TEST OF FAITH

When God's people go to him in prayer, he responds by either giving us exactly what we ask for or something even better. We have his promise on that. God is speaking to us when he says, "If you then, though you are evil, know how to give good gifts to your children, how much more will your Father in heaven give the Holy Spirit to those who ask him!" (Luke 11:13). Jesus' words remind us that what we need the most are the gifts the Holy Spirit brings: forgiveness and faith. But our prayers don't stop there, because he also invites us, "Call upon me in the day of trouble; I will deliver you, and you will honor me" (Psalm 50:15).

The Bible overflows with just such definite promises. When some believers in the early church had doubts about prayer's power to change the status quo, the apostle James chided, "You do not have, because you do not ask God" (James 4:2).

A TEST OF CHRISTLIKE LOVE

Our inclination is to use prayer to gather in a bounty of God's blessings for ourselves. And surely he wants us to pray for the things we want and need. But the prayers of a mature Christian are also quite selfless. God's Spirit, working in our new-man hearts, changes us—perfects us. As we grow, we begin to turn more of our attention to the needs of others. The change that is taking place in our hearts is also changing the way we view other people. In fact, we are changing so much that we will even begin to include our enemies in the prayers we bring before God.[1]

Hanging from a cross, Jesus uttered the most unlikely of prayers: "Father, forgive them [those people who are crucifying me]" (Luke 23:34). Jesus' example on Calvary is a lesson for us. In prayer God gives us a way to express our Christ-like love for someone who is committed to despising us. Even if he or she has rejected our outward expressions of kindness and Christian love, we can still pray for an enemy (Romans 12:21). The enemy can't stop us. In the end, our prayers may be the only way to show love to the folks who see themselves as our enemies.

PRAYER IN CHRISTIAN SCHOOLS

Christian education takes prayer seriously. The Christian education model teaches children that prayer empowers them. With prayer, they can make a real difference. They learn that they can pray to God anywhere, at any time, and he will listen. They learn to pray with other Christians to seek God's blessings. And they learn to pay attention to the blessings they receive as a result of their prayers.

Jesus said that anyone who has faith the size of a mustard seed can move mountains. What parent wouldn't want his or her child to learn to pray at a very early age so that this marvelous resource would be available throughout the child's life?

DISCUSSIONS FOR CHAPTER NINETEEN

1. How can parents teach their children to have a healthy and vigorous prayer life?

- Are the important lessons about prayer better taught at home or at school? Explain.

2. How can prayer satisfy a human need to do something that has eternal consequences?

---

[1] We'll have more to say about the role prayer plays in our human relationships in the fourth and final part of this book, which discusses the Christian education understanding of *love*.

3. React to this statement: *God answers our prayers by giving us exactly what we ask for or something even better.*

4. Has God ever had to say to you, "You better let me do that before you make a real mess of things"? Explain.

5. Read Matthew 7:7; Matthew 26:41; 1 Thessalonians 5:17; Isaiah 58:9; and John 15:7. What new insights were added to your understanding of prayer from these texts?

• What important lesson(s) regarding prayer do you want your child to learn at home and teachers to reinforce at school?

CHAPTER TWENTY

The Headwaters of Joy

Have you ever taken an inventory of the emotions you have experienced in life? Most of us have had real-life experiences with fear and anger. We know the feelings associated with loneliness, confusion, jealousy, grief, or embarrassment. But how about *joy?* Have you ever been filled with so much joy that you thought you might explode?

In this chapter we will consider the origins *(headwaters)* of our joy as God's people. Our conversation will consider *why* and *how* the Christian education model encourages students to celebrate their blessings with *joy* of biblical proportion.

WHY CELEBRATE?

There are lots of reasons for celebrating. Developmental psychologists have, for example, identified play as one of the most satisfying causes for human enjoyment. An *Aha! moment* can produce feelings of great joy, as can a performance that demonstrates a high level of skill. Young people experience the joy of competition. Winning is a cause for pumped fists flung wildly into space and high fives all around. Losing? Maybe not so much. But let's not forget that losing is an important part of the game. Without the possibility of losing, winning has no meaning. So it might even be possible to talk about a *celebrated loss,* though the tone of such a celebration understandably would be a bit more muted than if the team had won.

Older folks get a kick out of watching their kids or grandkids compete, but they can also celebrate the joy of a quiet moment of solitude and reflection. We celebrate the completion of a difficult task or the accomplishment of something that is particularly noteworthy.

We take a break from our normal routines to celebrate personal milestones—birthdays, anniversaries, baptisms, graduations, weddings—or to celebrate group accomplishments. Some events, like picnics, simply celebrate the joy of being together.

Our celebrations highlight the good things that have happened in our lives. Some are the results of personal initiatives (like graduations). For others (like birthdays), we may have done absolutely nothing to harvest the joy of a special day for celebrating.

The first chapter of the Bible describes how God's creative power brought everything we know into being. But three words often get lost in the excitement. These three words report the very first interaction between God and his human creatures. The Bible says, "God blessed them" (Genesis 1:28).

The intent couldn't be clearer. The author of Genesis (Moses) was taking an inspired editorial position, declaring that God's blessings are the headwaters for all our joy. Nothing has changed in the millennia that have passed.

Everything we have is a blessing from our heavenly Father. With food and drink, shelter and security, family and friends, work and rest, he blesses us. Physically, emotionally, and spiritually, he blesses us. Because of sin, humanity's attitude toward the gift giver has changed. God's love drives him to continue to pour out his blessings on the entire human race, even though we have collectively cursed him and murdered his Son.

CELEBRATING GOD'S BLESSINGS

It is part of our design to celebrate the things we enjoy. As Christians, we celebrate God's blessings whenever and wherever we worship him.

At a basic level, worship *is* celebration. It is an exercise of our sanctified will. Because of the Spirit's work of transforming our hearts to align with God's will, we can make choices that please God. Our worship flows from hearts filled with so much gratitude that we cannot help but thank God. And the beauty of it is that we can worship God when we are alone in the privacy of our own thoughts or we can worship him together with other Christians.

Some expressions of worship are consciously planned, others just happen. In fact, everything we do can be viewed as a celebration that is carried out in the spirit of worship. It can occur when we are walking the dog, playing basketball, or washing a load of socks and underwear.

Every family can relate to the hurried lifestyle of contemporary family living.[1] Home worship of the planned variety can be a difficult proposition. All

---

[1] The pace of life in a school setting these days is just as frenetic as it is in the home setting. The pace of life has quickened in every setting over the last few decades.

parents admit that their family's devotional activity is hampered by busy schedules and unexpected interruptions. But we also know that there are underlying factors that make the hurriedness of contemporary living an easy excuse for neglecting family time with God and his Word.

In practical terms, the major obstacle is not a shortage of time but the real culprit is *discontent,* which is the antithesis of thankfulness. When we no longer remember the source of every blessing, when we stop saying thank you to God every day for the blessings he has given us, we have crossed over into the dangerous swamp of discontent. Lacking a healthy *gratitude attitude,* it is almost impossible to devote time at home to any kind of God-pleasing worship.

In our culture the concept of thankfulness seems a bit out of whack. Our production-based economy may have to shoulder some of the blame. It shuns contentment. Progress is always measured in terms of *more.* The message comes through loud and clear in the media. At a very early age, children learn to be dissatisfied because plenty is never enough. They are programmed to want more things, more prestige, more success, more experiences, more of life, more money, more acclaim, more, more, more. Coupled with that is the false notion that we get ahead in life by hard work and the sweat of our brow.[2] Please do not misunderstand; the value we place on hard work is very high. The problem comes when we convince ourselves that everything we have is the result of our own effort or that we are entitled to everything we have. God is the author of all good gifts. Everything we have comes from the loving hand of a heavenly Father, who promised to meet all of our needs.

So, if we live in a culture that fosters a never-ending drumbeat of discontent, *when, where,* and *how* do Christians rediscover contentment?

The cancer of discontent grows when we count our blessings only in physical and material terms or when we believe the myth that what we have is the result of our own cunning or hard work. The Christian's source for contentment is found in a tiny baby born two thousand years ago in the flyspeck on the map called Bethlehem. Contentment comes to us in the form of an ugly cross and an empty burial chamber. Jesus is a gift that satisfies. He is the living fulfillment of those three overlooked words in Genesis. He is the blessing of all blessings.

---

[2] Sociologists are sounding a new alarm these days for a generation that sees itself as entitled to be treated as royalty. The cultural phenomenon is a new, magnified level of narcissism that far surpasses the narcissism of the 1980s—the so-called Me Decade. The antithesis to such narcissistic behaviors is simple humility and common contentment.

The hurried home doesn't have to be hurried. The demand for more doesn't have to rule us. We already have everything we need.

Contentment is a lesson that children need to learn at a very early age. It is a lesson that moms and dads need to teach on a daily basis so that it is never forgotten. The Christian education model is committed to revisiting this concept at many junctures in each child's educational development, but the basic concept of contentment needs to be modeled at home from the very beginning. We need to talk frequently with our children about the physical, emotional, and spiritual gifts that God pours out daily for us to enjoy. We need to find opportunities in the daily schedule of the home or the classroom to stop and say thank you to God.

THE JOY OF WORK

Understanding that God is the source of all of our blessings changes our perspective on work. The so-called *Judeo-Christian* work ethic—when correctly understood, taught, and modeled—can be summarized in a simply stated principle: *Our work is first and foremost an offering to God.* If that sounds like religion-speak, be assured it isn't. God has a huge stake in our workaday lives. He gives meaning and purpose to our work. He provides the time, opportunities, skills, and the wits for us to carry out our work-related tasks. Whether our jobs are to make corporate decisions or to count hex nuts on an assembly line, the work we do is an extension of the first job God gave to man, which was to *take care of* Eden. We're working for the Lord now. The great joy of it is that we don't have to work to win our heavenly Father's approval. Jesus has already done that. We work to show him how grateful we are. So, with the daily grind comes the joy of praising God and giving glory to his saving name.

Across the board, God-fearing moms and dads want their children to become independent. (See 1 Thessalonians 4:11,12.) They understand that children need to learn how to work, and they are concerned about grooming a healthy work ethic in their children. The Christian education model takes its signals from God's Word, presenting human work as a thank offering to God and a way of giving glory and honor to his name. ▪

DISCUSSIONS FOR CHAPTER TWENTY

1. How does your family celebrate special occasions that mark family milestones?

- How does your family celebrate national holidays?

- How does your family celebrate religious holidays?

- How does your family celebrate life in Jesus?

- Why is the *how* of celebrating important?

- Why is the *why* of celebrating even more important?

2. Why is it so easy in our culture to take God's blessings for granted or even to begin to believe that all we have comes from our own hard work?

3. How can Christian schools teach the joy of work?

4. How can Christian parents teach children that all of their hard work is dedicated to giving glory to God?

5. Read Psalm 81:16. What kind of blessings from God's hand does this psalm seem to be talking about?

- Read Matthew 6:33. How does Jesus help us put our priorities into their proper perspective?

- As a result of studying these Bible passages, what important lesson do you want your child to learn at home and in school?

CHAPTER TWENTY-ONE

Sabbath Joy

Anyone who has ever pulled a double shift knows that no one can keep working without a break. It is impossible to talk about our work lives without eventually considering the need to rest. But the idea of taking time off from our daily grind was not conceived in the mind of man. In his own divine way, God also works. Resting from one's labor was his idea.

Of course, God doesn't tire as you and I do. But by positioning his activity as *work,* God has blessed us with a precedent that deals with our human need for rest. In this chapter we will examine God's approach to providing rest for the weary on three levels: physical, emotional, and spiritual.

A DAY DEDICATED TO GOD

You can find the first written record of work in chapter 1 of Genesis, where God's great work of creation is described in surprisingly vivid detail. We hear how light, sun, moon and stars, oceans and dry land, vegetation, birds, fish, and animals all came into being as God ordered, by the power of his spoken word. We also learn how God lovingly gave Adam and Eve the gift of life, each in a unique way. When God stepped back to evaluate his work, he declared that all of it was good.

And then God *rested.*

This is a very revealing statement, because God didn't need to rest. He took a break from his creative work for our benefit, to provide an example for us. He wanted us to know that while our work is a blessing, so is the rest he gives us from our work. Now note the timing. The idea of a Sabbath rest existed before sin spoiled everything. In Eden, Adam and Eve were blessed by both their work and their rest; God deserves all the credit for giving both. After they were cast out of the garden, their work and their need to rest from their work would become an ongoing cause for turmoil and resentment. The temptation to elevate either one's work life or recreational life to the status of a false god is a constant challenge. Yet God continued to provide for his sin-stained human creatures with the blessings of both.

OBSERVING THE SABBATH DAY

As time went on, God revealed more about how he wanted his people to observe these periodic breaks from their labors. At Mount Sinai, God defined the pattern for this rest period. One day in every seven was to be a day dedicated to the Lord. God's people were expected to treat this day as sacred. Everything about it was to be a memorial to God's goodness.

Today we refer to Sabbath law as the Third Commandment: "Observe the Sabbath day by keeping it holy" (Deuteronomy 5:12). The curriculum used in the Christian education model includes the teaching of this commandment.

The Third Commandment offers us relief from a brutal workload. Exhausted bodies and minds reclaim their vitality during this 24-hour rest period. But our heavenly Father was also addressing the need for emotional downtime. By declaring this day as a day of respite from our labors, God limited the distance people could walk on this special day of rest. Folks could not travel or transact business. Every Sabbath Day was spent close to home, where God's people could enjoy the fellowship of family and friends. Their emotional batteries could be recharged by an encouraging word from a neighbor or an opportunity to spend time with a family member who seemed discouraged.[1] Such was the nature of *church* in Old Testament times. God's revealed truth came to the people in the many pictures provided through the annual festivals and from the visual lessons expressed in the furnishings and ceremonies in God's tabernacle and later in the temple. Folks would go there to worship God with their sacrifices and their prayers. But the fellowship of God's people in the community brought rest to the worn-out emotions of hard-working people.

By attending to his people's physical needs with a day of respite from their labors and by addressing their emotional needs with a day spent within the community of friends and relatives, God was also leading them to see they had a need for a spiritual day—one that would bring peace to all. On the Sabbath everyone was to hear that their sins had been forgiven and to relearn the simple truth that God loved them. They were to gather together to hear God

---

[1] In our culture we have lost some of the benefits and blessings that God's people in Old Testament times enjoyed. The civil and ceremonial laws that limited travel and business transactions no longer apply to New Testament Christians.

speak to them in his Word, sing psalms together, and worship him with their prayers of thanksgiving and supplication. This worship usually happened in private homes, where there would naturally be strong social and communal overtones to the Sabbath.

Today God's weekly Sabbath is still dedicated to worshiping God. Children attending a Christian school and their parents are encouraged to regularly come together with other members of the *body of Christ* to find spiritual rest for their souls. By gathering for worship, they will be strengthened with God's promises for the challenges of the next week.

FORMAL WORSHIP

When two or three people gather together for any reason, there likely will be some disagreement about the *who, how, when, where,* and sometimes even the reason *why* they have gathered. We're human! Some of that disagreement is the result of temptation still lurking in our hearts. We are works in progress. Some of our tendencies to challenge one another come from having a free will. It's okay for each of us to have opinions. But public worship would be chaotic if each individual worshiped in his or her own way at the same time. Our omniscient God would be able to cipher what each individual was trying to express to him, but we would not be able to communicate well with one another. It wouldn't take long before everyone would be trying to out-shout everyone else.

Formal worship brings order to our public worship. Over time God's people have developed some very good templates for orderly worship. When connected with the Word and the sacraments, these templates are sometimes referred to as *liturgies.*[2]

Liturgical worship creates a sense of sameness and continuity from one week to the next. Worship in one church will not be exactly the same as one might find in another church, but it is likely that they will both make use of the same elements, which include an invitation into God's presence, a confession of sins, a reminder of God's forgiveness, hearing God speak through his Word, celebrating the sacrament together, praying together, and receiving God's blessing.

Christians the world over identify with certain days in the year. These festival days focus on key elements in the story of our salvation. Christmas, Easter, Jesus'

---

[2]Some churches call these templates their *worship agendas.* Others refer to them as *orders of service.* These terms mean the same thing; they are all used to describe the community's plan for group worship.

ascension into heaven, and Pentecost are at the top of the list. They recall moments in human history that have eternal consequence for us all. God's people mark their calendars (and their lives) accordingly.

Christian schools celebrate the Sabbath Day by encouraging parents to attend worship services weekly with their children. Students and their parents are also invited to join other believers for special worship opportunities to observe church festivals that commemorate key events critical to our understanding of our faith. Children are taught that worship flows from a heart of gratitude and appreciation for all that God has done for us, not from a heart driven by obligation or social conscience.

Children may occasionally be asked to participate in public worship in specific ways (singing, for example) that will more fully engage them in worship.

DISCUSSIONS FOR CHAPTER TWENTY-ONE

1. What important message do parents convey to their children when they take them to church every week?

- What is the message that is being sent when parents do not bring their children to church?

2. Discuss the pros and cons of the practice of some Christian schools to keep a record of weekly church attendance for each student.

3. Read Hebrews 10:25. What blessings from God do we refuse when we stop attending public worship services?

- What are some of the most common reasons for not attending church regularly?

- How can Christian parents overcome these temptations?

✝

The face of wickedness and evil just doesn't seem to change. Greed, violence, bloodshed, extortion, hatred, dishonesty, envy, deception, and a host of other evils have dogged our race throughout history. But one thing has changed. We've changed; our hearts have changed. Because of our faith in Jesus, you and I look different to the rest of the world. So do our children. The gospel has changed our appearance. We think, talk, and behave in ways that are noticeably different from the way unbelievers think, talk, and act.

The power God uses to change us is his love. The difference that others see is the way we treat one another and them. We love others. At full spiritual maturity, we love others even more than we love ourselves.

Christians are God's ambassadors to a world still living in the darkness of unbelief. Jesus said people would know we are his disciples *if we love one another.* In a world that can hardly be described as *loving,* you and I are his boots on the ground—difference makers—following in the footsteps of the greatest difference maker of all times. Love is our only weapon. We are the cup that carries the cool water of the gospel to folks dehydrated by spiritual thirst.

When asked about the criteria they plan to use to choose a school for their children, a surprising number of parents say, "I'm looking for a school where my child will be loved." These parents know that the student-teacher relationship is a key factor in the learning process. They understand that there is a connection between nurturing and loving. When teachers love their students and students love their teachers, the best kind of learning can occur.

PART
FOUR

"Now we see but a poor reflection as in a mirror;
then we shall see face to face.
Now I know in part; then I shall know fully,
even as I am fully known.
And now these three remain: faith, hope and love.
But the greatest of these is love."

1 Corinthians 13:12,13

CHAPTER TWENTY-TWO

The Circle Expands

The lad had convinced himself that he was an aspiring NFL quarterback. He dropped back into the pocket, faked a handoff, and threw long to an imaginary receiver. The ball was a flattened relic from the '80s. I dug a few crumpled bills out of my pocket. "Here, kid, buy a new football."

The boy's response caught me by surprise. "Aw, I don't need a new football, mister. I just need my grandpa to throw it to." As we lobbed the pancake back and forth, I learned that the boy's grandfather was in the hospital. I wondered who needed the other more, the boy or his grandpa?

We are born into this world needing others and wanting to be needed by others.

YOUR CHILD'S FIRST CLASSROOM

A newborn depends on very few people. At first there is just the infant and his or her mother—a relationship initially rooted in biology. Their connection has been more physical than anything else. The mother nurtures; the growing fetus depends on her for its minute-to-minute nourishment. A more fully developed emotional attachment will come later.

Soon the circle expands to include the infant's father. If there are siblings, they will become a part of the widening circle. In time it will include grandparents, aunts, uncles, and cousins. Here, in the family environment, children learn the values of compassion, honesty, contentment, optimism, sharing, hospitality, and a work ethic. Here children learn to pray and begin to acquire the most basic Bible truths. Describing the most valuable learning real estate on earth, one church leader wrote:

> The critical location for Bible teaching is not the classroom but rather the household: the walk, the sitting together on the porch, the snuggling together in the warmth of bed, the joy of rising to a new day. In life Bible truths begin to have meaning for the whole

person. For every one of us the Christian home is the first and foremost center for spiritual learning. And this kind of learning is rooted not in education, but rather in the socialization process. A child learns God's truth in much the same way in which he learns to talk.[1]

DEPENDENCY AND CHILDLIKE HUMILITY

Eventually the child will learn to relate to playmates. When formal education begins, the circle expands once more to include teachers and friends. As the circle widens, children become less dependent on those who once occupied the center of their restrictive world. By the time they hit puberty, many are sending strong messages to their parents that their time to break free has arrived.

Adolescents see adulthood as their lifelong ambition. For a child, being an adult means freedom from controls that have been imposed since their young lives began. Most of us have forgotten what childhood was like.

Jesus' disciples were wrestling with trying to understand their relationship with him. They saw him as their ticket to being close to power, whatever that meant in their own limited views of his work. Perhaps they thought their association with Jesus could lead to having more control over their own lives. Their idea of greatness was connected with having the power to rule one's own destiny. Finally, one of them found the courage to ask the big question: *Who is the greatest in the kingdom of heaven?*

Jesus was prepared. He asked the master of the house where they were staying to send a little tyke into the room. Jesus wanted his disciples to remember their growing-up years. They were men now, steeped in the ways of the adult world. They saw themselves as independent adults, who were more or less in control of their lives. They had forgotten what it was like to be a child.

Soon a toddler stood before them. He was barely able to walk or talk. He also lacked any legitimate claim to greatness. The lad had no money. No job. No education. No experience. No authority. No pedigree. No physical strength to speak of. No royal title. No valuable possessions. No impressive body of knowledge. No plan. No academic degree. No skills. No special connections. No unique powers. No notoriety or fame. No resources of any kind. In plain English, the kid was *a nothing—a nobody*—completely reliant on others to sustain, support, and nurture him. In short, he was a *dependent.*

---

[1] "Teaching to Cognitive and Affective Outcomes," an unpublished manuscript by Joel Gerlach.

The lecture began. "I tell you the truth," said Jesus, "unless you change and become like little children, you will never enter the kingdom of heaven. Therefore, whoever humbles himself like this child is the greatest in the kingdom of heaven" (Matthew 18:3,4).

The disciples were puzzled. *Unless you change?* Change what? It took a moment for Jesus' message to sink in. Words like *unless* and *never* are hard to digest and impossible to dismiss. Were they hearing Jesus correctly? Had he said that if they didn't *become like this child,* they might as well give up, that God's kingdom was beyond their reach? The disciples' confidence in their own eternal futures must have been shaken by Jesus' words. Why would a loving God make it so impossible for them to enter his kingdom?

In the history of the world, some kingdoms have been truly remarkable. A handful left footprints we still admire: the Roman Empire, the Persian Empire, the Ming Dynasty, the Aztecs, Egypt—the land of the great pharaohs—the Mongolian Horde, the British Empire, etc. Great sovereigns often ruled with iron fists. Perhaps the disciples wondered if Jesus was speaking about the heyday of David and Solomon, when the united kingdoms of Judah and Israel were a mighty national force.

Adults pursue another kind of kingdom. In our day-to-day lives, we invest our time and energy in our work. Our kingdoms have names like *medicine, law, business, the marketplace, politics, agriculture, commerce, technology, education, government.* Mature adults carve niches, climb corporate ladders, and set goals to build these kingdoms. These kingdoms matter to us. Sometimes they matter too much.

Privately we engage in building another kind of kingdom that is mostly about *me.* It is constructed on the false foundations of *my* talent, *my* career, *my* honor, *my* status, *my* image, *my* legacy, *my* identity, *my* influence, *my* ideas, *my* wits, *my* successes, *my* intellect, *my* perspective. We work hard at perfecting this kingdom. It is unabashedly ego driven. There's very little humility here. We protect it, defend it, flaunt it, enlarge it, control it, refine it. Some of us would die for it if necessary. This kingdom can become god-like, mastering us and undermining our spiritual integrity.

The young child standing before the disciples knew none of these kingdoms. He had not given even the most casual thought to building one. He was happy to be nurtured, supported, and loved by his parents. He was genuinely humbled by his status as a child, unashamed and unembarrassed by the knowledge that he depended on his parents for everything. In a word, he was *dependent*. Yet, ironically, he lived like a king.

You and I need the humility of that child. So do our children as they grow to become adults. We hear the truth about our status in Scripture and drop to our knees in humble repentance. We are entirely dependent on God for his mercy. Daily we turn to our heavenly Father to provide whatever we need to be physically, emotionally, and spiritually satisfied. He wants us to come back every day for whatever we need. He promises that it will be there. And it is. But here's the kicker: none of this would be possible if our divine provider didn't love us.

God wants us to recognize how much we need him. He wants our trust and confidence. He wants us to depend on him for everything. It gives him joy. It is his way of proving over and over that he loves us.

AN OUTRAGEOUS ILLUSTRATION

Before we leave this powerful image of that child standing shyly before the disciples, we must consider one other aspect of Jesus' lesson. Jesus said, *"Unless you . . . become like little children."* Does this strike you as a cockeyed notion? Such a thing is clearly outside the scope of human experience. If Jesus Christ had not said these words, they would have been dismissed as the words of a fool or a madman. In the entire history of our planet, not a single case has ever been reported of an adult miraculously returning to his or her childhood. Not one. It's like the virgin birth or being born again. Anyone with an ounce of sense knows it just doesn't happen.

Even more shocking, because such a thing is humanly impossible, Jesus' message could lead us to despair. Taken at face value and given the biological facts, heaven would be out of reach for us. None of us has the power to return to the time when we were children. We've all swallowed the poison of adulthood. Building kingdoms is what we do. And many of us do it with immense passion and zeal. We've been conditioned to think that the rewards for building our personal little kingdoms will somehow last and matter. It's just not humanly possible to turn back the clocks of our lives to times when we were still so young and naive.

And that is Jesus' point. Only God can do the impossible. What we cannot do, he does for us.

Through the miracle of God's Holy Spirit, we can become like that humble little child. In childlike humility, we can relearn how to rely on God's charity and goodwill for everything we need. The model of Christian education has the audacity to plant the seed of spiritual humility into the hearts of the children we serve. Christian education teaches children to rely on God's loving providence for their physical, emotional, and spiritual sustenance. No other educational philosophy in the world can make that claim. ■

DISCUSSIONS FOR CHAPTER TWENTY-TWO

1. Reread the quotation from the beginning of the chapter (pages 122,123). Do you agree that spiritual learning is rooted not in education but in the socialization process?

2. The introduction to this chapter makes reference to the expanding circle of human relationships every child experiences during the first two decades of life. How wide is the circle of relationships in your child's current life stage?

3. Are there personal kingdoms in your life that threaten to rule your heart and your life?

   • How do our earthly kingdoms threaten the kingdom that Jesus wants us to have?

4. How can Jesus' teaching about childlike humility lead Christian adults and children to some healthy wrestling matches with God?

5. Read Luke 22:24-30 and John 13:1-17. What is the connection between loving others and humbly serving others?

   • Why is it so important for us to see from these two texts that Jesus practiced what he preached?

- Do you agree or disagree with the following statement? *The best way to teach humility to a child is to model it in your own personal life.*

- As a result of this discussion, what important lesson do you want your child to learn at home and at school?

CHAPTER TWENTY-THREE

Vested With Authority

Her name was Hannah, Hebrew for *passion*. When the Bible introduces Hannah to us, she has already spent many years yearning for a child. We are told that the Lord himself closed her womb. Yet Hannah persisted in praying that God would change his mind and give her a child.

One day when Hannah came to God's house to worship, she lost control of her emotions. Weeping, she began to pray, "O LORD Almighty, if you will only look upon your servant's misery and remember me, and not forget your servant but give her a son, then I will give him to the LORD for all the days of his life" (1 Samuel 1:11).

An old priest named Eli overheard her emotional prayer and mistakenly concluded she was drunk. As he began to admonish her, Hannah explained that she was distraught because she was barren. Eli understood her anguish and promised to pray that the Lord would grant her a child.

Not long after, Hannah gave birth to a son. She named the boy *Samuel*. When the youngster had been weaned, Hannah kept her promise and brought him to the old priest, asking Eli to educate her son and prepare him for a life of service. Thereafter Hannah visited Samuel each year, bringing a beautiful new robe for him to wear.

This moving narrative reminds us that children truly are an extraordinary blessing. But the ancient scene we just witnessed is not as rare as one might think. At the beginning of every new school year, a similar scene is repeated thousands of times when young parents bring their children to school for their very first day in a classroom. You can feel the tension as moms and dads coax their little ones into a room filled with other children and then quietly walk away. The separation is often traumatic. Parents instinctively know their child's young life will never be the same. In this chapter we will strip away some of the raw emotions of this pregnant moment to examine what is really happening when a parent walks a child over the education threshold for the first time.

THE FOURTH COMMANDMENT AND AUTHORITY

With every child, God provides resources that moms and dads will need for carrying out their new parenting role. Many young parents, for example, report a maternal or paternal instinct that they had never noticed before. Others feel the weight of a new burden of responsibility. They privately wonder if they have the right tools for raising a child.

God's Word discusses a parent's role with clarity. In Proverbs 22:6, Solomon wrote, "Train a child in the way he should go, and when he is old he will not turn from it." In Ephesians 6:4 the apostle Paul addresses God-fearing dads directly: "Fathers, do not exasperate your children; instead, bring them up in the training and instruction of the Lord."

The Fourth Commandment says, "Honor your father and your mother, as the LORD your God has commanded you, so that you may live long and that it may go well with you in the land the LORD your God is giving you" (Deuteronomy 5:16). This is the first commandment in the Decalog that speaks specifically about our human relationships. Its position suggests that God intended the parent-child relationship to be understood as primary.

Luther helps us grasp the nuance of that opening word *honor* by connecting it to *authority*. In the explanation to the Fourth Commandment, he explains that we are *not to dishonor or anger our parents and others in authority, but we are to honor, serve, and obey them, and give them love and respect*. It is also noteworthy that the word *author* is the root word for *authority*. The first meaning for the word *author* is *originator*. In the Fourth Commandment, the author of all things—the *originator* of all creation—is indicating that he is sharing some of his divine authority with parents. He also promises that those who honor, respect, and obey such God-given authority will prosper.

When God blessed Hannah and her husband with the gift of a child, he also gave them the authority to make decisions that would affect young Samuel's life. As parents, they rightly exercised this newly acquired authority when Hannah turned Samuel's care and instruction over to Eli. Hannah and her husband must have had a lot of trust in the old priest. Remember, Hannah had yearned for this child for many years. Young Samuel was the apple of her eye and the most valuable treasure of her life. What confidence she must have had in old Eli's love for children! How she must have trusted that God would bless Eli's work as he taught the child to be honest, kind, respectful, industrious, and all of the other character traits that any God-fearing parents would want for their child.

EXERCISING AUTHORITY WITH LOVE

By an extension of the Fourth Commandment's emphasis on parents, God has also vested a share of his authority in other human roles: kings and queens; presidents, governors, and judges; lawmakers and law enforcers; boards of control, CEOs, and people in supervisory positions; justices of the peace and ordained ministers; ships' captains, military officers, and airline pilots; jailers and jurors. There are, no doubt, thousands of elected, ordained, and appointed roles in our society to which God has assigned a limited portion of his divine authority. God gives these folks a share of his authority out of love for the people they are expected to watch over.[1] Teachers are included in his list. When a parent walks a youngster through a classroom door, that very act implies that the parent is willing to share some of his or her God-given parental authority with the child's teacher(s).

THE SHEPHERD-KING MODEL

History books are filled with stories about people who abused their authority. Tyranny has no place in the home, nor is there any room for it in a classroom. The key to exercising the authority that God has entrusted to parents, or teachers, is best captured in a beautiful four-letter word: *love*. When the exercise of authority is rooted in selfless love, tyranny will not be a part of the equation.

We get snapshots of tyranny and the rank abuse of power from the Bible's narratives that describe Israel's kings. Only a handful of them knew how to exercise their God-given authority with justice and mercy. Only a few demonstrated unconditional, sacrificial love for the people they ruled. The majority were unfit to rule. Some were dishonest or cruel. Others worshiped false gods, leading their subjects away from the God of their salvation.

David was Israel's greatest king. During his reign, many of the hostile, idol-worshiping, neighboring nations that surrounded God's people were subdued. David established Jerusalem as the capital and designed a great temple that would one day be built to God's glory. During the last half of his 40-year reign, King David became very powerful.

---

[1]God is so committed to maintaining order that he has said that he even wants us to honor and respect people who have done a terrible job of exercising their authority. When Jesus was asked whether it was right to pay taxes to the Roman caesar (a ruler who could be incredibly callous and cruel toward his subjects), he said, "Give to Caesar what is Caesar's, and to God what is God's" (Matthew 22:21).

On the other hand, David was hardly the picture of godly integrity. Some of his kingly decrees betrayed pride and a self-serving attitude. He abused his authority and committed terrible crimes against God and his own countrymen, including adultery and murder.

But there was another side of David that deserves our attention. For one thing, David was courageous beyond belief. He trusted that God would be with him in battle. As a boy, he had tended his father's flocks. More than once he had put his own life on the line to defend the sheep. As a young man, it was David who volunteered to go head-to-head with a giant named Goliath. David slew the more than 9-foot tall monster with nothing but a stone and a sling.

There's something else about David that we need to see more clearly. David loved God. He was a prolific writer of verses dedicated to the Lord. (We know these verses as *psalms.*)

In spite of ungodly behavior as king, David had a heart of gold. When his own rebellious son Absalom died trying to overthrow his own father, David wept bitterly. "O my son Absalom! My son, my son Absalom! If only I had died instead of you—O Absalom, my son, my son!" (2 Samuel 18:33).[2]

Scripture says that God viewed David as "a man after his own heart" (1 Samuel 13:14). This is significant because the New Testament gospels refer to Jesus as the *Son of David,* not the son of Abraham or the son of Jacob or Moses. Jesus himself used the picture of a tenderhearted shepherd-king who wields his power for the good of the sheep he loves. Speaking of himself, Jesus said, "I am the good shepherd. The good shepherd lays down his life for the sheep" (John 10:11).

This is important because Jesus is the King of our lives. He doesn't merely rule the universe; he rules in our hearts. As he reminded his disciples, "All authority in heaven and on earth has been given to me" (Matthew 28:18). God has entrusted sheep like you and me, and little lambs like your child, to the Good Shepherd's tender care and keeping. He has promised to exercise all of his cosmic authority in ways that will always be tempered by his boundless love for us. Beyond that, he wants Christian parents and Christian educators to exercise their God-given authority in exactly the same way, with selfless love for Jesus' little lambs.

---

[2]David's deep sorrow over Absalom's unsettling death pictures for us God's sadness over mankind's rebellion and his offer to become our substitute in death for people who really don't deserve it.

In a memorable section of Scripture, the apostle Paul helps us understand what godly love is supposed to look like:

If I speak in the tongues of men and of angels, but have not love, I am only a resounding gong or a clanging cymbal. If I have the gift of prophecy and can fathom all mysteries and all knowledge, and if I have a faith that can move mountains, but have not love, I am nothing. If I give all I possess to the poor and surrender my body to the flames, but have not love, I gain nothing.

Love is patient, love is kind. It does not envy, it does not boast, it is not proud. It is not rude, it is not self-seeking, it is not easily angered, it keeps no record of wrongs. Love does not delight in evil but rejoices with the truth. It always protects, always trusts, always hopes, always perseveres.

Love never fails. (1 Corinthians 13:1-8)

This is the kind of selfless love that Christian parents and Christian educators strive for when they are exercising their limited share of authority that God has vested in them. ▣

DISCUSSIONS FOR CHAPTER TWENTY-THREE

1. How does the idea that God has shared some of his authority with parents, who, in turn, share some of their God-given authority with their children's teachers, argue for a strong parent-teacher partnership?

2. Give an example of how authority could be abused by either a teacher or a parent.

3. Reread 1 Corinthians 13:1-8. Talk about how to put these verses into practice at home and at school.

• *Love is patient.*

• *Love is kind.*

- *Love does not envy.*

- *Love does not boast.*

- *Love is not proud.*

- *Love is not rude.*

- *Love is not self-seeking.*

- *Love is not easily angered.*

- *Love keeps no record of wrongs.*

- *Love does not delight in evil.*

- *Love rejoices with the truth.*

- *Love always protects.*

- *Love always trusts.*

- *Love always hopes.*

- *Love always perseveres.*

- *Love never fails.*

CHAPTER TWENTY-FOUR

Echoing the Music of God's Love

This intriguing little gem recently appeared on the Internet: *Those who danced were thought to be quite insane by those who could not hear the music.* Think about it.

Love is a lot like the unheard music of this quotation. Most people think they know what love is all about. We've experienced the love of a child, a parent, a friend, a spouse, a mentor. We know the emotions often associated with love.

The ancient Greeks had no less than three words *(eros, phileo,* and *agape)* to describe this human phenomenon. Each word reflected a distinct understanding of love's intrinsic meaning.

The biblical truth is that only those (adults and children) who have heard the music of God's unconditional love—a love that forgives without any strings attached—have the fullest understanding of this four-letter word. In English we call such unencumbered love *grace. Grace* means "undeserved or unearned love." It expresses the idea of being fully and freely loved without an expectation of giving love in return.

The unbelieving world looks on with curiosity (and sometimes with malice) as it observes believers dancing to the tune of God's gracious love, and it concludes that Christians are all quite insane. The unbelieving world hasn't yet heard the music.

CHRIST *FOR US*

The Christian's musical ear of faith is always tuned to hearing what Christ has done *for us.* God's Word points to the sacrifice Christ Jesus offered up on the cross *for us.* Baptism provides a daily reminder of our kinship in God's holy family and the eternal peace the Savior has won *for us.* Weekly sermons in church and Bible studies proclaim a Redeemer who lived *for us.* The Lord's Supper offers us Jesus' own body and blood, given and shed *for us.*

Jesus for us is very good news for condemned sinners. We call this good news the *gospel.*

The message of Christ *for us* is where every Christian's understanding of love has its origin. But it is not where our understanding of love ends. The same gospel that tells us about God's great love *for us* also changes us. And this change is a radical kind of change that is quite obvious to others. How you and I love our neighbors is a direct reflection of how Jesus conducted his life on earth.

Jesus' passionate love for people is anything but ambiguous. For Jesus, love is never just a word; it is an action, a behavior, a way of life. Love permeated everything he said and did when he lived among us. He healed the sick, restored sight to the blind, and shed tears of sorrow for the dead. He listened to people and hurt when they were hurting. He had compassion on the mute, the forgotten, the dying, the lonely. And he is outspoken in urging us to follow his lead—to be salt and light to a world rotting in sin and perishing in darkness, to offer a cup of cold water, to give up our cloaks, to visit the imprisoned, and to feed the hungry.

"Love each other as I have loved you," he says (John 15:12).

Children attending a Christian school learn to pray for a fellow student who has had an accident or is ill. They exercise their faith by offering to help a friend who is struggling to understand a new academic concept. They make an effort to encourage one another in their faith walk. They look for opportunities to demonstrate Christlike compassion for people who are discouraged or hurting over a loss. Their motivation for such behavior is the good news of the gospel, which reassures them that God loves them unconditionally for Jesus' sake.

IMITATING CHRIST

As we (and our children) grow in faith, we become more like Jesus. We imitate his love. The apostle Paul wrote, "Be imitators of God, therefore, as dearly loved children and live a life of love, just as Christ loved us and gave himself up for us as a fragrant offering and sacrifice to God" (Ephesians 5:1,2).

It's usually about this time in the conversation when someone notes that there are lots of great people whose lives we could imitate—great humanitarians like Gandhi, Mother Teresa, or Albert Schweitzer. Why limit ourselves to the Jesus model?

The challenge is worth considering. These people, and others like them, represent wonderful examples of compassion. There is a lot we can learn from them. They deserve our admiration and respect. But the objective truth is that they were all flawed. To have God's admiration and respect, they needed to be perfectly in tune with his holy will. Since the fall, that distinction has belonged to only one person. Jesus' heavenly Father declared, "This is my Son, whom I love; with him I am well pleased" (Matthew 3:17). A just and holy God could never have said that about Gandhi, Mother Teresa, or Albert Schweitzer because it would not have been true. They were not perfect in every way. God's Son was right with his heavenly Father in every way. He lived the perfect life and offered himself as the perfect sacrifice for sinners like us. Jesus is the perfect *love model*. In a Christian school, the model your child will be taught to emulate is the model of Jesus as he taught and ministered to people while he lived here on earth with us.

PERSONAL BURDEN BEARING

The concept of burden bearing was captured well in the iconic Boys Town statue of an older boy with a younger boy draped over his shoulders. The inscription reads, "He ain't heavy, Father . . . he's m' brother." One quick look at Jesus bleeding and dying and anyone can readily see that he was 100 percent committed to bearing our burden of sin.

In love, the same Savior extends the privilege of sharing another's burdens to each of his *imitators*. He emboldens us with the knowledge that whenever we flex our muscles to shoulder another person's burden, we are serving him. "Whatever you did for one of the least of these brothers of mine," he said, "you did it for me" (Matthew 25:40).

The unbelieving world's compassion can seem to mirror the actions of Christians, but unbelievers cannot be motivated by Jesus' love for them because they do not know, by faith, who Jesus is or what he has done for them. This is an important distinction between secular educational models and the Christian model. Secular schools cannot motivate their students with the love that Jesus demonstrated by willingly going to the cross. Public school teachers cannot legally use the classroom environment or their school's curriculum to teach their students that Jesus cares about them.

A HIGHER KIND OF COMPASSION

When we think about bearing one another's burdens, some might imagine themselves rolling up their sleeves and getting to work in a food pantry or filling sandbags along the banks of a mud-swollen river. For others it might mean pushing wheelchairs, sitting for long hours holding someone's hand, sending cards or e-mails with encouraging messages, running summer camps for mentally handicapped children, or counseling fragile people. These are acts of godly compassion. But at its pinnacle, burden bearing is about filling others up with hope.

Folks who are carrying heavy burdens are often searching for answers to life's most difficult problems. They are looking for the kind of encouragement that helps them stand up to the pain or fight back the tears of loneliness. God's people not only take the time to listen so that we will know where others hurt, we also offer God's most powerful answers to their suffering.

The most satisfying answer to the hardships of life is the hope-filled message of salvation in Christ Jesus. It is the good news of the cross and our incredibly beautiful relationship with the bearer of that cross. In Jesus, mankind's burdens are made lighter. He is our brother, ever willing to carry that portion of the load that we ourselves cannot carry. He carried our greatest burden—sin—to the cross.

In our era, the opportunities to share Jesus with a hurting world seem to be growing exponentially. God has placed us into this time and place for a reason. We are here to share the story of the crucified and risen Christ with the troubled, the fragile, the lonely—with anyone who is living without hope.

TEACHING COMPASSION

There's no place like home for teaching compassion. Kids learn first about what it means to be a loving and giving human being as they observe their parents and siblings caring for one another. When Christian parents follow Jesus' example, they are already living within the parameters of the Christian education model.

In Christian schools, instructors teach children about God and his love for sinners. In the Christian education environment, learners grow as individuals who enjoy serving their Savior by serving others. Faithful parents and Christian teachers work together in tandem to shape the attitudes and worldviews of children. As their children mature, moms and dads will see them beginning to live with the same compassion that Jesus had for those who could not help themselves. ▪

DISCUSSIONS FOR CHAPTER TWENTY-FOUR

1. Share an example of something your child has said or done recently that already demonstrated growth as a compassionate person.

2. Give an example of what love looks like when there are *strings attached* (meaning that it is based on some condition).

3. How does personal burden bearing help to proclaim the good news of Jesus to a world still living in the darkness of unbelief?

4. Read Luke 10:25-37. What lesson did Jesus want us to learn from this parable?

   • Discuss strategies that can be used at home and at school for teaching compassion.

CHAPTER TWENTY-FIVE

Intervention at the Cross

Children sin. For parents who know their children well, this may be stating the obvious. We do not like to believe it of our own kids, but we all certainly have ample opportunities to observe it. We know this is true because we know ourselves all too well. We know the darkness that lingers in our own hearts and how we've learned to cover our trails when we have sinned. Our children, however, don't often see the sin in our lives. Just as parents often prefer to view their children as the pictures of innocence, many children regard their parents (or their teachers) as incapable of committing sin. In general, most adults work hard at promoting this myth.

Sin is a frightening reality of the human experience. And it should be communicated in just that way. The full reality is that sin's worst consequences are too hellish to imagine. Sin undoes the goodness that God wants to bring into our lives. It corrupts the human soul and ruins the perfect image the Creator wants us to have. Sin distorts the truth and undermines God's righteous will. It moves us to rise up in unholy rebellion against our holy and loving God. It spawns hatred, greed, and injustice. It puts us at odds with nature, destroys our communion with one another, and diminishes our perception of self. Worse, our sins have shattered the idyllic relationship that the human race was originally created to enjoy with its heavenly Father. It may not always be easy or comfortable to talk about sin, but it is necessary. You and I need to discuss it with our children and with one another. We have a responsibility for generating a full-blown, ongoing conversation about sin with our children—both its reality and its devastating and inevitable consequences.

Our talks about sin with our children will remain abstract and meaningless unless they see us standing in the shadow of the cross. It is important, for example, for them to hear us confess in public worship: "I am by nature sinful. I have disobeyed you in my thoughts, words, and actions. I have done what is evil and failed to do what is good. For this I deserve your punishment, both now and in eternity." And it is just as important for them to observe our relief and joy at knowing that our sins have been absolved in the never-ending stream of Jesus' forgiveness. Our children will know exactly where to go with their sins when they see us go to the cross with ours.

CORRECTION AND ADMONITION

Gentleness and kindness are touchstones of our faith. Gentle people avoid confrontation at almost any cost. "Blessed are the meek," said Jesus, "for they will inherit the earth" (Matthew 5:5). It's not surprising then that so many of us shy away from admonishing a person caught up in sin, even when the situation clearly calls for it. We confuse avoidance with kindness and gentleness. We struggle with admonition because we know our own hearts so well. We look at a fellow Christian trapped in a cycle of sin and temptation and conclude, "I'm hardly the one to admonish him. I am no better." And that could very well be the truth.

Coming from someone who lacks a humble and contrite spirit, admonition is ill advised. Who would listen? Without humility, admonition comes off as pure arrogance—judgment driven by an attitude of self-righteousness.

Jesus said that we should make sure to remove the huge wooden plank from our own eyes before attempting to take a tiny splinter from someone else's eye (Matthew 7:3-5; Luke 6:41,42). What practical advice for would-be admonishers!

Godly humility needs to be tempered with the confidence that we have been washed clean in the blood of the Lamb. This is one of the great paradoxes of the Christian life. We are at once humbled by our sin and confident of God's forgiveness. Both are needed for correcting a wayward believer's course in life.

Loving admonition makes a child of God aware of the spiritual danger he or she is in. The Bible tells us to speak the truth in love (Ephesians 4:15). A sinner who is unable to face the truth of his or her own sin is hopelessly mired in denial, a spiritually deadly form of denial at that.

Bible truth consists of two important facts. The first is the fact of sin. The fact of sin makes us unacceptable in God's presence. Our holy and righteous God despises sin, and his perfect sense of justice demands that he punish sinners. The second fact is that God has, through the work of Christ Jesus, wiped our slates clean. He tells us how he did this in his Word. In Scripture we learn that we are forgiven, completely and fully. With God's forgiveness we are reinstated in God's family as though nothing ever happened to interrupt our cherished relationship.

Sometimes we have difficulty admitting our sin. Either we don't want to give up our pet sins or we are unable to accept our sins as a matter of fact. In either case, the end result is the same: unbelief! It happened in the case of Pharaoh (Exodus 10:1). It happened to one of Jesus' disciples, a man named Judas (Matthew 27:3-5). It can happen to us or to our children. To deny our sinfulness is to remain unrepentant.

Given this tragic outcome for a heart that has become hardened by sin, it is easy to see why patient and loving admonition is such an important part of the Christian life. An unbroken cycle of sin amounts to spiritual strangulation. When a friend (or a son, a daughter, a student) remains unrepentant and is caught in a cycle of sin and temptation, you may be the only person in a position to do anything about helping that individual break the cycle. God uses the fellowship we enjoy with other believers to bring an erring brother or sister, father or mother, son or daughter face-to-face with the deadly reality of sin. In so doing, Jesus says that a "sheep" which has lost its way can still be saved from its own foolishness.

A BIBLE MODEL FOR GODLY INTERVENTION

King David, you may recall, had committed a whole series of sins, including lust, adultery, deception, conspiracy, and murder. (See 2 Samuel 11.) He was knee deep in a cover-up. And, as he later admitted, he was tormented by a guilty conscience. Though David was a God-fearing person, he was stuck in denial. And his denial was directly connected to an unrepentant heart. David was in grave jeopardy of falling into unbelief, and he was approaching the point of no return—when one's heart becomes so hardened to sin that all hope for repentance has evaporated.

In love God intervened, sending his prophet Nathan to confront David with the deadly spiritual consequences of his sins. The prophet's approach was direct. When David finally saw the wretched condition of his own sinful heart, he was filled with remorse, and he knew where to go with his sins. In one of his most quoted psalms, David prayed, "Cleanse me with hyssop, and I will be clean; wash me, and I will be whiter than snow" (Psalm 51:7). The repentant king sought pardon from his Savior-God and freedom from the burden of his guilt. The Lord reassured David that he had been forgiven and was restored to favorite-son status.

Children can get caught in the revolving door of temptation and sin. They are not often guilty of heinous felonies, but many children wrestle with the temptation to lie, deceive, or manipulate. Sinful patterns develop quickly for kids. Sins that are not corrected when children are young can lead to serious spiritual pathologies.

A wealthy young man once asked Jesus what he needed to do to be saved. Jesus told the young man to sell all that he had and give the money to the poor. It was Jesus' way of sending a wake-up call to the man, warning him that he was in grave danger of losing his own soul because he was caught in the sin of greed. The man turned and sadly walked away. His heart had become so hardened by his love for money that even Jesus' wake-up call didn't penetrate.

Love strips away all the excusing and ignoring of sinful attitudes. In Christlike love we may need to be brutally honest with a fellow believer who is trapped in a cycle of sin and living on the brink of unbelief.

The Christian education model teaches children to humbly and lovingly intervene when a fellow believer is trapped in a tangled web of sin and living on the edge of unbelief. Christian schools teach the biblical concept that we must speak the truth in love to bring a straying believer back to the cross. This call applies to parents, teachers, and students.

Families need to talk about sin on a regular basis. So do teachers. Christian education promotes *four Rs:* READING, WRITING, 'RITHMETIC, and the only *R* that has eternal consequences—REPENTANCE. The underlying purpose for our talks about sin is not to teach one another how to look better in public, it is to create daily opportunities to be reassured that God has fully and completely dealt with the dark condition of our sinful hearts. Our purpose is to daily remind children, and one another, that we are, for Jesus' sake, forgiven. ▪

DISCUSSIONS FOR CHAPTER TWENTY-FIVE

1. Make a list of cycles of sin and temptation that children can get caught up in.

2. What did Jesus mean when he said that you must remove the beam of wood from your own eye before you can help someone else remove a speck from his or her eye?

   • How is the beam in your own eye removed?

3. How did God intervene on our behalf?

- What is distinctively different about an intervention strategy that is employed in a Christian school and one that we might expect to find in a secular school when it comes to intervening in sinful behavior?

4. Is there a right way and a wrong way to *speak the truth in love?* Explain.

5. Is there a difference between correcting a child for breaking house rules or classroom rules and breaking one of God's commandments? Explain.

6. Read 2 Samuel 12:1-23. From the details of Nathan's intervention strategy, what might we learn?

7. What do you admire most about Nathan's approach to correcting King David?

- What lesson(s) from this example of the right way to intervene could you see yourself applying to a situation in which you know your child has sinned?

CHAPTER TWENTY-SIX

God's Children and Jesus' Great Co-Mission

Forty days after Jesus shattered death's enslaving chains, he gathered his disciples on a mountaintop. It was time for him to return to his heavenly home. Before ascending into the clouds, he had one final lesson to teach. It was a lesson he had taught many times before, but never in such a direct and concise manner.

He began the lesson by reiterating that the Father had given all authority in heaven and on earth to him. Then he exercised that divine authority with orders from headquarters:

"Go and make disciples of all nations, baptizing them in the name of the Father and of the Son and of the Holy Spirit, and teaching them to obey everything I have commanded you. And surely I am with you always, to the very end of the age." (Matthew 28:19,20)

These words are called the *Great Commission.* They present a formidable challenge for Christ's church on earth. They serve as our personal marching orders.

The great *co-mission* is the reason for our very existence.[1] It calls on all of Jesus' followers to work hard to grow his kingdom. In real life that can translate into painful sacrifices. It sounds difficult, complicated—a logistical nightmare—a hard task to wrap one's head around. But the message itself is remarkably simple. In fact, Jesus once told his disciples that to have eternal life one must only *know God.* (See John 17:3.) The Great Commission calls on us to make sure that as many people know God as we can possibly reach.

---

[1]Luther said, "We live on earth for no other purpose than to be useful to others. Otherwise, it would be best for God to take our breath away and let us die as soon as we are baptized and have begun to believe. But he lets us live here in order that we might lead others to believe, doing for others what he has done for us. To serve my neighbor and to serve him best of all by bringing him to Christ, this is, in fact, the primary purpose of my continued existence" (*Luther's Works,* SL 9, page 968).

PASSING THE TORCH

Stated or unstated, all educational models see the *passing-of-the-torch* as a critical element of their mission. Christian education is committed to passing the light of life on to the next generation. We each have an important role to play in God's eternal plan. This includes our children.

The apostle Paul put our Great Commission role into perspective with four penetrating questions. These questions provide a step-by-step strategy for carrying out the mission we've been given:

1. *How can they [unbelievers] call on the one they have not believed in? (prayer)*

2. *How can they believe in the one of whom they have not heard? (faith)*

3. *How can they hear without someone to tell them? (make disciples)*

4. *How can anyone tell them unless they are sent? (commissioned by Jesus) (See Romans 10:14,15.)*

Christian classrooms need teachers to pass the torch of Jesus' saving gospel on to their students. Christian homes need parents to ignite that living torch of faith in the hearts of their children through the miracle of Baptism and to make sure their faith in Jesus continues to burn brightly. Christian churches need preachers to equip God's people for the work they have been called to do.

God's call has gone out to every generation since Adam and Eve first received the simple promise that he would send an offspring to crush the serpent's head. Our children must be handed that torch so that it can shine brightly for their generation. And then their generation will need to pass it on to the next.

The task before us right now is to prepare our young people to take over when our work is finished. They are God's ambassadors to their own generation. He wants them to be ready.[2]

PERSONAL EVANGELISM

My first missionary journey was neither complex nor well planned. An eight-year-old doesn't know much about constructing strategies for reaching

---

[2] In 2 Timothy 4:2 we sense the urgency for being well prepared when Paul writes to his young protégé Timothy: "Preach the Word; be prepared in season and out of season; correct, rebuke, and encourage—with great patience and careful instruction." The seasons Paul is referring to may be a reference to life stages. Children can be stellar models of missionary zeal.

out to the lost with the gospel. My Sunday school teacher invited each child in the classroom to bring along an unchurched friend the following Sunday. I took *unchurched* to mean anyone whom I had never seen in church.

The only unchurched kid of my own age in the neighborhood was a nine-year-old named Roberto. Roberto used words that church members are not supposed to know—another clue regarding his *churched* or *unchurched* status.

Roberto and I seldom talked. Eight-year-olds don't have a lot to talk about. But our paths crossed daily as Roberto ambled home from Brown Street Public School and I negotiated my way home from Cross Lutheran School. Occasionally one of us would lob a friendly snowball at the other during the winter months. Every now and then, in summer, we traded baseball cards or shot marbles. Now there was this challenge from my Sunday school teacher. Roberto was my target.

I don't recall how I worded my invitation. It was probably something brief and to the point. Nor do I remember Roberto's response. I only know that the following Sunday I walked to the house where I thought Roberto lived. The narrow stairwell leading to his family's apartment smelled like mothballs. Roberto was waiting for me, dressed in a clean, white shirt and wearing a tie. His mother could barely speak English. She greeted me warmly and kissed Roberto on the cheek. Then she sent the two of us on our way with a cheerful *buenos dias.*

That's all I have left of this childhood memory. I wish I could report that today Roberto is a baptized child of God and an active church member. It would be nice to be able to recall sitting together with him in church or Sunday school. I can't. Nor do I know if someone from the church followed up with a visit to Roberto's mother. I know I didn't. I don't even remember if Roberto and I ever did much together after that Sunday morning. Too many years have passed.

I do know that something important happened in my own story on that day. I learned that nothing brings me greater joy than telling someone about Jesus. I have learned since to be patient when someone shows interest in hearing about my faith in Jesus. I've learned how important it is to be an active listener. I've learned to be persistent in following up with people who are searching for meaning and hope. I've learned that the conversations I have with others are so much richer when I take the time to cultivate meaningful relationships.

COMPLETE JOY

The apostle John wrote, "We proclaim to you what we have seen and heard, so that you also may have fellowship with us . . . to make our joy complete" (1 John 1:3,4). The stories that the apostle enjoyed retelling were his own eyewitness accounts of a bloodstained cross and an empty tomb. It was John's story as much as it was Jesus' story. He knew these stories had the power to change people's lives.

John's joy is also our joy. You and I know about the peace we have with God and our certain hope of eternity in heaven with Jesus. The thrill of sharing that knowledge with others makes our joy in this life even more profound.

Our children will experience the same joy when they are led to understand that God has a role for each of them in his grand disciple-making *co-mission.*

The Christian education model teaches children to till the soil and sow the seeds of faith, even while they are young. They learn early that their lives have meaning and purpose because God has a plan for using them to accomplish his ends. They quickly come to understand that no matter what occupation they choose in life, they have a higher calling into a lifetime vocation of being Jesus' ambassadors to a world still living in the dark. They know that the most loving thing one human being can do for another is to introduce him or her to the Savior.

GOOD NEWS ON A BREEZE

Jesus once said, "The wind blows wherever it pleases. You hear its sound, but you cannot tell where it comes from or where it is going" (John 3:8). The gospel travels like the wind. It takes wing according to the divine will of God's Holy Spirit. But God's Spirit does not always travel in a straight line. Nor does he move according to the whims and wishes of men. We can't predict where or how the Spirit will work his miracles of faith. We do not always get to see the results of our planting efforts. And we certainly have no control over the success of the harvest. We are here to plant. Our children are part of the Spirit's ongoing harvest. The fields of our generation are ripe for the harvest, and we have work to do right now, before the night comes when it will no longer be possible to do God's work. That work includes preparing our children for carrying out their part in God's Great Co-mission. ▪

DISCUSSIONS FOR CHAPTER TWENTY-SIX

1. Have you ever had an opportunity to tell someone about Jesus? What happened?

2. What implication does Jesus' Great Commission have for the role of a Christian parent?

   • What implication does the Great Commission have for the Christian educator's role?

3. Read John 17:3. What kind of knowledge is the torchlight of life that all Christian parents and teachers want to pass on to the next generation?

   • How will we carry out this great assignment?

4. Imagine your child as a married adult with several children. What kind of parent do you think your adult son or daughter will become?

   • How prepared will he or she be for the Christian parent's role?

5. TRUE or FALSE: *One never retires from being a parent.*

   • TRUE or FALSE: *Your influence in your child's life will last only a few years.*

   • Discuss your responses.

6. Read Mark 4:30-32. In this parable Jesus was making a prophecy regarding the remarkable growth of the New Testament church.

How do you think the church grew from such a tiny "mustard seed" to such a large "plant"?

• What privileged role do all of God's people share when it comes to participating in his Great Commission?

• When did God call us for doing this work?

• What is your plan for teaching your child about his or her important role in Jesus' Great Commission?

• How can Christian educators teach this lesson to the children in their care?

CHAPTER TWENTY-SEVEN

The Bottom Line

The Bible is profoundly real when it comes to telling us the truth about ourselves. It never minces words when speaking about sin, death, temptation, or the hopelessness of the human condition. At the same time, it always presents God's solution in terms that are just as tangible. While the end of the Bible's story is undoubtedly about our future in heaven, everything else is earthbound.

Christ's cross was firmly anchored in the terra firma of a hill called Calvary. Executions were held on this otherwise insignificant speck of useless terrain. It had a reputation as a place of unspeakable inhumanity. Jesus came to this very spot to deal with our greatest need. And he accomplished everything he came to do.

Clothed in human flesh, Christ lived among us for three decades. One of the great expressions of the Christian faith summarizes the humiliation of his incarnation like this: "[He] was conceived by the Holy Spirit, born of the virgin Mary, suffered under Pontius Pilate, was crucified, died, and was buried."[1] In other words, he was human in every sense of the word. He got hungry and became tired. He felt such great sadness that he sometimes shed tears. We also know that he experienced the heartache of economic hardship. He rubbed elbows daily with people who struggled with poverty. He visited the markets where people bought, sold, and haggled on the basis of value and according to the law of supply and demand. He lived in a world not so different from our own, where everything had a price and nothing was free. Before we consider the cost of a child's education, it is good to once more consider the cost of our own salvation. God's promise of life in heaven is, without question, the most precious thing we own. It became ours at a terrible price, yet it cost us nothing. The price God paid for our souls was incredibly high; it cost him the life of his only Son.

[1] From the Apostles' Creed.

FISCAL REALITIES

The basic economic realities that existed in Jesus' day still beg for our attention today. School systems must deal with fiscal issues daily, just as each of our families has to deal with its financial obligations.

Education has always had cost implications. During his three-year ministry as an itinerant rabbi, Jesus' little traveling school was a shoestring operation at best. He was obviously not in it for the money. On at least one occasion, he reminded a would-be disciple that foxes have holes and birds have nests, but the Son of Man had no place to lay his head. Yet, there were mouths to feed— 12 strapping men. Jesus had himself called them to study under his tutelage. He had to shoulder some of the responsibility for caring for their earthly needs. So, Jesus' rabbinical school (the Bible sometimes just calls them the Twelve) relied heavily on the gracious offerings of those who supported his cause.

In our lifetime the cost of education has escalated dramatically. The trend is likely to continue. Christian schools have no choice but to deal with economic realities.

FUNDING EDUCATION

Public education is supported by tax dollars. Private schools, on the other hand, rely heavily on tuition fees to support their programs. Many private schools operate on a *for-profit* basis.

Christian schools, sometimes referred to as *parochial schools,* may either be supported entirely by church donations or through a combination of donations and tuition fees.[2]

Some states have voucher systems that make tax dollars available to help fund private or parochial schools. A charter governs this educational model. It is also not uncommon for public, private, and parochial schools to seek philanthropic third-source grants or loans to support special programs or projects.

The cost of owning and operating a Christian elementary school or high school expands the parent-teacher partnership to include other Christians who have a vested interest in supporting a Christian school program. These donors are motivated to support their church's local educational programs out of grat-

---

[2] The majority of schools operating in the WELS system fall into this latter category. Most elementary schools in the WELS are owned and operated by local congregations that support their schools with gifts and donations, as well as through tuition. With a few exceptions, WELS high schools are owned and operated by federations consisting of local area congregations.

itude for all that God has given them. Many have themselves experienced the blessings that came from attending a Christian school at some point in their lives. Their generosity is an example of selfless sacrifice.

Educators who teach in a Christian school setting also make significant sacrifices in terms of both time and income. They consider it a privilege to teach children about their Savior, even if their choice to serve in the Christian education environment has a negative impact on their personal income. These individuals deserve our deepest respect for their devotion to the Christian education model and its mission.

A WORTHY SACRIFICE

The Bible gives us a snapshot of one godly family that lived in a tiny village named Bethany. This family consisted of three adult siblings—a brother named *Lazarus* and two sisters named *Mary* and *Martha*. Bethany was located just a couple of miles outside the city gates of Jerusalem—about a two-hour hike from the temple mount. It seems that Martha, Mary, and Lazarus supported Jesus' ministry with their private donations. They also opened their home to Jesus and his disciples. It served as a place for escaping the hostile attitudes of the temple leaders who were opposed to Jesus' message. It is likely that Rabbi Jesus taught some of their friends and neighbors in the security of their home. Their hospitality was commendable. Jesus loved all three of them dearly. The Bible includes several wonderful accounts about these three friends of Jesus. To make our point, we are going to concentrate on Mary's attitudes regarding Jesus and his ministry.

For starters, the Bible describes Mary as a dedicated student, deeply devoted to learning more about the good news that Jesus had come to share with his followers. Though the term that we have been using throughout this book *(Christian education)* would not be invented for another 1,400 years, Mary was one of the very first advocates for Christian education. In one Bible narrative, we find Mary sitting at Jesus' feet, listening to him teach. (See Luke 10:38-42.) Unlike Martha, who was distracted by the earthbound concerns of entertaining friends and being a good hostess, Mary made a conscious decision to focus on what her Lord Jesus had to say. She understood that her faith would mature as she grew in her understanding of his message.

Mary's teacher noted that her decision to sit at his feet was the right choice. He called spiritual learning the *one thing needed*. Then he added that the truth she held in high regard would not be taken away from her.

Sometime later, in an emotional moment, we see Mary seeking comfort at her Lord's side after her brother, Lazarus, had died. Jesus was himself moved to tears by Mary's overwhelming sense of grief and loss. With compassion, and using the power of his divine Word, Jesus called Lazarus back to life. (See John 11:1-44.)

Perhaps the most telling story of Mary's heart for hearing Jesus' saving message occurs in John chapter 12, verses 1-11. Once again the scene is the home of these three siblings. The three have decided to give a banquet in Jesus' honor. True to character, Martha is bustling about. Lazarus is reclined with Jesus at the table, engaged in a conversation. He too is interested in learning more about God's plan for the remainder of his life. The disciples are there as well. The Bible does not tell us if Mary is acting on impulse or if she had been contemplating this for some time. In either event, Mary enters, carrying a container of pure nard—perfumed spice mixed with olive oil. Without a word of explanation or concern for the cost of what she is about to do, Mary splashes the oil over Jesus' feet. Then she begins to gently spread it with her own hair. Soon the delicious fragrance fills the room, and all the guests enjoy the heady scent.

Jesus again acknowledged Mary's devotion. Her sacrifice was a wonderful example to those who were present. Mary had her priorities right. Her worshipful act of anointing Jesus' feet with valuable perfume showed her great love and admiration for Jesus.

The beautiful profile of this woman's faith serves as the ideal. It explains why parents and Christian educators make such great sacrifices for the children that God has placed into their care. Like Mary, we make sacrifices because we love our Lord Jesus. Our devotion demands self-expression. We honor him with our sacrifices.

One of the best ways for us to express our gratitude for his sacrifice is to commit ourselves to making the sacrifices that will assure us that our children have every opportunity to hear about Jesus and his great love for them. But we also make these personal sacrifices because we love our children. For the majority of us, godly parenting is the most unselfish thing we will ever do.

Done with godly motives, Christian parents are first and foremost engaged in Jesus' Great Commission to go and make disciples of all nations. As we ourselves begin to resemble Jesus' disciples, we are hard at work *discipling* our children. With hearts changed by Christ's love for us, you and I gladly give up our precious time, our last ounces of energy, and our hard-earned dollars so that our children will be with us in heaven someday.

DISCUSSIONS FOR CHAPTER TWENTY-SEVEN

1. Create a comprehensive list of the values or benefits that God's people enjoy through Christian schools.

   • Have you personally experienced some of the items on the list?

2. Do you have a family plan aimed at teaching your child how to approach the matter of sacrificial giving to support the ongoing ministry of Christian education?

3. How do Christian parents sacrifice their time or their energy for the sake of their children?

4. Many Christian schools have access to funds that are designed to help low-income families make use of their school program. Invite a church leader or a school administrator to explain if there is such a program in your congregation and, if so, how it works. If such a program does not exist, try to learn more about how such a fund might be started.

CHAPTER TWENTY-EIGHT

Children Are a Blessing

Dear Parent,

Repeat after me: *Children are a blessing.* When kids have been typically obnoxious for the last 10 miles in the backseat of your van on the way home from school, whisper it under your breath: Children are a blessing. As summer days with the kids wear your patience thin, write this down where you can see it several times a day: Children are a blessing. When the science project is due tomorrow and you just learned about it tonight, tell yourself once more: Children are a blessing. When you fear it will be necessary to rent a bulldozer to clean your child's room, practice saying it again: Children are a blessing.

Dear Teacher,

Please say this together with me in unison: *Children are a blessing.* When group members can't get along during their play periods because fair play still needs a lot of work, say the magic words: *Children are a blessing.* When you're convinced someone is lying about how the chameleon found its way into Dorthea's desk, say a prayer that begins with these words: *Children are a blessing.* When you've lost sleep over Terrence because he daily challenges your authority and saps all your energy, try to recall these sacred words: *Children are a blessing.*

There are challenges when it comes to nurturing children. One learns over time and from experience to expect the unexpected. How are you supposed to react when your blessing belches out loud in the middle of a church service or asks for money for the eighth time in a week and its only Tuesday? Blessings aren't supposed to talk trash, mouth off, curse, gossip, profane, or undermine authority. Blessings don't fight, cheat, or look at porn. Except that these blessings do. Children arrive fresh from the womb with sin in their hearts. These blessings have a way of angering us, disappointing us, even hurting us. The joy of having children is often tinged with heartache, sadness, and frustration. So, really, how can parents and teachers see kids as blessings?

GOD'S PURPOSE FOR GIVING YOU THE GIFT OF A CHILD

To begin, the reminder that each of these blessings comes from God should give us pause. We need to consider how to treat each of these special blessings in a way that will honor the gift giver.

There's an old saying, often spoken with tongue in cheek: *You don't get to pick your relatives.* Actually, there's a lot of homespun truth in that axiom. It certainly applies to our children. But for God's people, it is true only in a good sense. Each of these little gifts is uniquely chosen for each individual parent. God has a purpose in mind as he makes the choice for us. This mom needs laughter in her life; that's why God sent baby Robert. Maria will one day tell her grandma about Jesus. God had that purpose in mind for Maria's life before he created the world. Little Allen will not have a very long life. But his premature death will cause his grieving father to seek comfort from God's living Word. The Word will bring his father's dead heart to life. And Allen's father will spend eternity with his Savior . . . and Allen.

When they first arrive, these little blessings seem so needy. In the first stage of life it is hard to imagine they might have anything of value to offer us. The relationship appears to be one-sided and sort of one-dimensional. We feed, nurture, provide, support, protect. They sleep, eat, and poop. Parents seem to be far more of a blessing to their children than the other way around. Give it time. Someday you will see how much you have needed your child, even when that little tyke was once completely dependent on you for his or her minute-to-minute care. One day you will know that the words *children are a blessing* have a lot more meaning when you say them without a hint of sarcasm. The big question is, *What will you do with this remarkable gift?*

A PARABLE ABOUT STEWARDSHIP

We began our conversation about Christian education with a parable from our master teacher. It seems only fitting to end with another.

> A wealthy businessman was scheduled to leave for an extended business trip. Prudent businessman that he was, the man wanted to make sure that all of his investments would continue to produce

dividends while he was gone. He called his three best managers in and challenged them to be the best stewards that they could be. To the first he gave five talents of silver. To the second he gave two talents. And to the third manager he gave one talent. Then the businessman left, confident that his assets would increase.

When the businessman returned, he was happy to learn that the manager who had been given five talents invested wisely. Now the original sum was worth ten talents. The second manager told his boss a similar story. The yield on the investment he made had also doubled. Then it was the third manager's turn to report. "Sir," he said, "you are going to be so proud of me! I was wise in recognizing that you wouldn't want to risk taking a loss on the one talent you gave me, so I buried it in a hole to keep it safe."

The businessman was incensed. "You are a wicked, lazy man who knows nothing about business. I was expecting some earnings from the talent I gave you. Give me the talent so that I can give it to someone who will know what to do with it. Get out! You're fired."

No, the parable is not about investing. It's not about children either. It's about gifts and how we care for the gifts God gives to us. It's a lesson in stewardship. But in the context of this book, it has a specific application for godly parents: treat your child with the dignity, grace, and respect that every gift from God deserves. Develop this gift's potential for growth with all the dedication you can muster. But remember, your child is on loan. Childhood lasts for only a few years. And those years fly by with such heart-pounding speed that most parents do not see the end coming until it is too late. These are the formative years—barely a handful of years—that God has given you to mark the direction of your child's young life. There are no Mulligans. No do-overs. You've got one talent to work with, or maybe two, or five. Go ahead. Invest. Show the boss what you can do. When you're working for God, your investments are all risk free.

AN ANTHOLOGY OF SMILES

Teachers collect things. This tired, old educator has collected ideas, stories, emotional moments, memories, observations. Stuff from the young lives of children I once taught. Stuff scribbled on shreds of old envelopes and yellowed note cards. Obscure stuff I stashed long ago in forgotten shoe boxes and bureau drawers now crammed with useless notebooks.

The other day I stumbled across an old scrap of an idea for a book—a wad of notes paper-clipped together. The promising title on the cover read "A Catalog of Smiles." I rifled through the pack like a kid flipping through a stack of Bazooka Bubblegum cards. What I discovered was an enchanting collection of anecdotes written by some of the children I had had in class. The educator in me cringed at the uneven grammar and the awful spelling, but this was truly the primitive kind of writing that authors crave because it was so transparent and honest. It was priceless: a childish prank, a tender moment between an 11-year-old and his grandma, kittens getting tangled in a basket of yarn, a moon-eyed girl looking for an excuse to talk with the boy of her dreams. One page contained a whole list of "Things That Make Me Giggle." It was pure gold: a slinky, butterflies, s'mores, licorice, clowns, stinky perfume. One mischievous youngster wrote, "I laughed out loud when my dad accidentally sat on a cactus." Another child remarked, "Jesus makes me happy." (I know just what she meant.)

Collecting and cataloging a book of smiles is an idea that still appeals to me. I can still close my eyes and imagine the smiles on the children's faces. They convey unfettered *joy*.

The learning process exudes joy. It is that special thing that happens when we know something today that we didn't know yesterday. Smiles are the rewards for *knowing* truth and for *being known* by those people who matter most in our lives.

Without using the actual words, the apostle Paul was the lead advocate for the learning model we call *Christian education*. Listen to the apostle's profound definition for the unique kind of *learning* that occurs in Christian schools: "Now we see but a poor reflection as in a mirror; then we shall see face to face. Now I know in part; then I shall know fully, even as I am fully known" (1 Corinthians 13:12). Saint Paul used the most important word in the entire vocabulary of Christian education. Twice. This word stands in sharp contrast to the twice-spoken *now*, which the world upholds as its fundamental educational currency. It is the little, four-letter word *then*. *Then* is what fuels the passion shared by parents and teachers who carry on the mission of Christian education. *Then* is when we will know God in all his glory. *Then* is when we will know the full embrace of a God who has known us from before the beginning of time. *Then* is when the Savior's anthology of smiles will finally be complete. And *then*, for eternity, we will celebrate the grandest of all graduations. ■

DISCUSSIONS FOR CHAPTER TWENTY-EIGHT

1. PARENTS: Share things your child has said or done to make you wonder if children are a blessing.

   • TEACHERS: Share things your students have said or done to make you wonder if children are a blessing.

2. PARENTS: Why do you think God gave the gift of a child to you?

   • TEACHERS: Why do you think God gave you the privilege of teaching students?

3. List ways that a parent or a Christian educator can *invest* in the gift of a child?

4. Read 1 Corinthians 13:11-13. What have you learned from this book that has influenced your approach to how you carry out your God-given role as a parent or as a Christian teacher?

   • Why is the final statement from verse 13 a fitting way to end our discussion about Christian education?